Visual
Merchandising
Principles and Practice

by Richard Carty

First Edition

MPC Educational Publishers
a division of Milady Publishing Corp.
3839 White Plains Road
Bronx, New York 10467

ISBN No. 0-87350-255-8

Text Designer — Gail H. Drillings

Illustrations — Shiz Horii

Contents

unit 4 — (continued)

unit 5 — The Components Of Visual Merchandising

unit 6 — The Structure Of A Visual-Merchandising Department

unit 7 — The Excitement And Challenge Of Visual Merchandising

Introduction

Visual Merchandising — Principles and Practice is a first-hand study of the visual approach to selling with emphasis on the how and why of display. As a basis for fully understanding contemporary visual-merchandising philosophy, a brief history as well as an organizational structure are included. The current methods of visual merchandising as well as the display layout of a store are also discussed.

The text has been divided into seven chapters. The first chapter is *a brief history of visual merchandising* up through the twentieth century. The second chapter deals with the *functions associated with different types of windows*. In the third chapter emphasis is placed on *interior display*. Chapter four discusses the *materials used in visual merchandising* while the fifth chapter concerns itself with *the components of visual merchandising*. The sixth chapter deals with *the organizational structure of a visual-merchandising department of a large multi-unit department store*. The seventh chapter presents *conclusions* and *a summary*. Chapter eight is inspirational It deals with *visual merchandising as an expression of art*.

Visual merchandising is a dominant factor in the selling process, and its future is bright due to the fact that merchandise does not sell itself. It is the job of the visual merchandiser to present the merchandise to the customer in the best possible manner so as to stimulate and increase sales as well as to create a desirable image for the store.

unit 1

A History
of Visual Merchandising

PRE-SEVENTEENTH CENTURY

Throughout the centuries, the most advantageous method for a person to sell his wares has been to exhibit them in such a manner that the prospective buyer is permitted a visual and tactile inspection of them. This elementary principle of merchandise presentation has persisted, intact, in Mexico, Africa, and India. In our society merchandise presentation has experienced a dynamic evolution due to changes in the culture, changes in the merchandise itself, and new merchandising philosophy as well as increased demands and sophistication on the part of the consumer. From its humble beginnings in the open markets and the hawking of one's wares, visual merchandising has grown to be an integral and dominant part of the selling process.

Mexican Open Market

Up until the seventeenth century, the masses were primarily concerned with their basic existence, and as a result they bartered for or purchased only the necessities of life. They did not need any stimulus to buy other than price competition. The lowest price point determined the purchase of goods. Luxury items were reserved for the wealthy.

SEVENTEENTH CENTURY

The seventeenth century was a decisive period because the middle class grew to a point where they had extra money to spend on non-staple goods, and the shop emerged as the normal place for them to spend this money. It was in these new shops that display had its real beginnings as a legitimate adjunct to the profitable merchandising of goods as well as establishing itself as an art form.

17th Century Shop

By the end of this century the word "shop" had evolved in meaning from an open stall in the marketplace or alley to denote the enclosed ground floor of a house which was used as the normal place for business. The counter itself and the business dealings had moved from the sidewalk to the interior of the shop.

The previously open windows were now enclosed with small panes of glass that forced shopkeepers to try a newer and less noisy manner of salesmanship. This was accomplished by an attractive display of goods on the shopboard in the window so the passing crowds would be tempted by the merchandise and be subject to what we now term impulse buying. This became the mode for selling the better-quality merchandise. These expensive display items usually involved merchandise newly arrived from the explorations of foreign lands.

This practice of window display became quite prevalent and was soon commented upon in the writing of the time. The reactions were both favorable and unfavorable. A Frenchman visiting London in 1663 had the following reaction:

> *There is no city in the world that has so many and such fine shops. For they are large and their decorations are as valuable as those of the stage. The scene is new everywhere and attracts the eye as we go along . . .*

During the eighteenth century the shop premises changed and improved, with the better shops taking advantage of plate glass for their windows rather than the small panes. The larger panes permitted the customer to see into the shops themselves.

By midcentury, many shopkeepers were experimenting with bow windows that projected out over the sidewalk and effectively caused the consumer to stop and notice the display. This was also a great innovation from a display standpoint in that it gave a whole new arena in which to exhibit merchandise. It increased the actual square footage to be used for display and changed the customers' viewpoint from merely a frontal one to a three-sided viewing area. This presented a new challenge to the shopkeeper in that he had to arrange his displays so that his merchandise would be viewable from all three sides.

Bow Window

By this time, display was becoming a technical art and display fixtures were appearing.

S. Von LaRoche described a typical window in *Sophie in London* published in 1786:

> *Behind the great glass windows absolutely everything one can think of is neatly, attractively displayed, in such abundance of choice as almost to make one greedy . . . There is a cunning device for showing women's materials. They hang down in folds behind the fine, high windows so that the effect of this or that material, as it would be in a woman's dress, can be studied.*

Prior to this time the prevalent philosophy was that any capital expenditure was for merchandise and not for fixtures intended to house or display the goods. However, socio-economic factors in the eighteenth century altered this thinking. New, higher-priced exclusive goods demanded a new type of merchandising presentation and the rising, affluent middle class came to expect such displays. This change in philosophy not only altered the appearance of the interiors of the shops, but gave birth to a new industry in terms of store fixtures. Daniel Defoe in the *Complete English Tradesman* took note of this phenomenon in 1732:

> *It is a modern custom and wholly unknown to our ancestors to have tradesmen lay out two thirds of their fortune in fitting up their shops. By fitting up I do not mean furnishing their shops with wares and goods to sell, but in painting and gilding fine shelves, shutters, boxes, glass doors, sashes, and the like, in which, they tell us know 'tis a small matter to lay out two to three hundred pounds.*

It is evident that by this time the shopkeepers had realized the value of spending money for fixtures and display to increase their return on investment in merchandise.

The foremost proponent of this new philosophy of visual merchandising was Josiah Wedgewood of "china" fame who, in 1765, opened a showroom in Grosvenor Square, England. Befitting the quality of the merchandise, he outfitted the entire showroom on an elaborate scale. He laid out entire dinner services, complete with all appointments, as if he expected dinner guests at any moment. These were changed frequently. His intention was to entertain his customers and give them a reason to return. He was a forerunner of what great stores like Tiffany's do with their china and silver departments in terms of the extremes to which they will go to have everything just right.

Display increased in usage and importance in the nineteenth century. Regardless of the size of the shop, some form of display was utilized. Whether it was a large or small shop, they were similar in that no one person was specifically assigned to the work of display. The owners did the work themselves or appointed one of their more talented salesclerks to attend to this function. Display was still not considered a full-time job or recognized as a profession.

19th century Shop

The equivalent of our modern discount operations appeared at this time in the London area. The drapers, as they were called, were primarily cash-and-carry people who operated on the basis of small profits and quick turnover. Their philosophy of merchandising involved price cutting and saturation display and advertising. They employed display to its maximum by filling their windows with merchandise and putting a price ticket on each piece. This was a practice unheard of at the time and soon came to be associated with a lower-end operation. No matter whether they were a discounter or regular-price shop, they still did their displays without the aid of a specialized person or department.

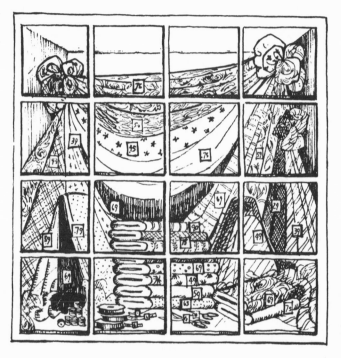

Ticketing

The nineteenth century saw the introduction and proliferation of mass-produced goods and a greater diversification of merchandise lines. Competition for the consumer and his dollar became more intense; purchasing basics was no longer the norm. By 1900 the need for professional display personnel was apparent to most stores. They began to hire such people or promote from within. The name "window trimmer" was given to these people because it was a correct description of their function. This was the real beginning of the job we know today as display or, more correctly, *visual merchandising.*

The stores realized the value of a proper presentation of merchandise, but they could not justify the expense of a person to do only this job. There were other duties associated with window trimming such as selling, stock work, and maintenance.

The window trimming was usually done after hours. The window trimmer had to be creative and ingenious because he or she did not have all the supportive people and materials that are available today. They were their own staff, their own fashion coordinator, and their own creator of props and fixtures.

TWENTIETH CENTURY

The twentieth century has seen the evolution of the window trimmer from a necessary addition to the selling function to one who, in a large multi-unit store, has a title such as VICE PRESIDENT FOR MERCHANDISE PRESENTATION or VICE PRESIDENT FOR SALES PROMOTION AND VISUAL MERCHANDISING. They now have large staffs that encompass many diverse types of people both in supportive and work functions. This executive is a part of the executive team. *The good display person has come to be regarded as an artist who practices a legitimate art form.*

Display as we know it today is, in reality, a recent innovation. Jerome Koerber of Strawbridge & Clothier, Philadelphia, who is called the father of interior display, was active around 1910. The days of the lonely window trimmer are gone. The term itself has been revised from display to the more encompassing term, "visual merchandising." It is no longer just a matter of making merchandise look attractive for the customer, it is the actual selling of the merchandise through a visual medium. *Selling is the job and responsibility of the visual merchandising department.*

Visual merchandising is held in high regard. Why? "It loves to make people happy," and this is partly what visual merchandising does. It creates interest and excitement in the merchandise and gives the customer the impetus to buy. The visual-merchandising department is an important part of the selling team, for it presents the image of the store to the customer and issues her an invitation to come in and shop. This function will grow in importance in the rest of this century because of various economic and competitive factors. The history of visual merchandising is really in its infancy. Its adult years will confirm it as a legitimate selling force as well as an art form.

FOR REVIEW AND DISCUSSION

1. What is the earlier meaning of the word "shop"?
2. What was the advantage of large plate-glass windows over the small-pane type that existed before the 18th century?
3. Why did higher-priced, exclusive merchandise demand more elaborate merchandising displays?
4. Explain why the job title, "Window Trimmer", was dropped in favor of "Visual Merchandiser."

unit 2

Exterior Display

THE FUNCTION OF WINDOWS

The first impression a customer receives of a store is from its exterior and its windows. They should be warm and inviting, with the intent of bringing the customer into the store to spend money. The windows act as a bridge between the exterior and the interior of the store by projecting the image of the store and showing its character and the quality of the merchandise carried. Whether it is a specialty store, department store, or discount operation, the windows tell a story to the customer.

The location of the store will determine the amount of space alloted to the windows. In the downtown area, where daily traffic volume is heavy and window shopping is important, more space will be devoted to windows. In a study of the window displays of fifteen major department and specialty stores in New York City, 32 per cent of the women passing by looked at the windows and 40 per cent of these actually stopped for a closer study of the merchandise.

STORE TYPE DETERMINES WINDOW TYPE

There are several other reasons for this fact, one being that the downtown store is usually the parent store and, as a result, carries the broadest range of merchandise. Another factor is that the downtown store has the staff to maintain all the windows. In the suburban stores, whether free-standing or in a mall, less space is given to the windows and more importance is placed on interior displays. This is due to limitations in size, store layout, and personnel. As an example, a prominent downtown Boston full-service department store has sixteen windows used for ready-to-wear presentations and twelve for home furnishings, while their largest branch has a total of six windows to be used for both areas.

A large specialty store in downtown Boston has twelve windows, six devoted to women's wear and six to men's wear, while their branches have an average of three. Discounters have few windows. These are in the front of their free-standing buildings and are used to post large sheet advertising of prices rather than merchandise. The interior is especially important to this type of store.

Chain stores utilize their windows in much the same manner as the department stores. Regardless of the type of store or location, it is the individual interpretation of the display and the store philosophy that determines the execution of the display and the store image that is created.

CLASSIFICATION OF STOREFRONT STYLES

All stores are limited by the types of storefronts and windows available. There are three basic variations of the front of a retailing establishment: straight, angled, and arcade. Store philosophy, image, and budget will determine which is the most appropriate for the individual store.

STRAIGHT FRONT

The most common and the most workable is the straight storefront. It runs parallel with the sidewalk, with the entrance being the only interruption in the straight line. The doorways

Straight Front

12

are either flush or slightly recessed. This effectively limits the number of display windows to the space where the traffic volume is the heaviest.

Slightly recessed entrances produce a foyer effect and provide additional display space in two shadow boxes. The front windows are flush with the building and permit the customer a frontal, one-sided view of the merchandise. The large corner window area is the focal point of the front and should always display the most important merchandise. The corner window permits a two-sided view of the merchandise as well as receiving double exposure from the passing traffic.

Straight storefronts usually appear where the building is enclosed on both sides by other buildings.

Corner Window

Angled Front

THE ANGLED FRONT

The angled front is merely an adaptation of the straight front except that the entrances are deeply recessed to create a lobby effect. The windows are at an angle to the sidewalk and act to draw the customer into the store. The advantage of this front is that in the case of a small store with a short front, it increases the total window area. The windows themselves are smaller in scale than in the straight front.

THE ARCADE FRONT

The arcade front is the least utilized of the three. The store will usually have several entrances which are recessed from the street with a glass-enclosed display area in the middle. This allows the merchandise to be seen from three sides and sometimes all four. Certain national chain specialty stores have made extensive use of this type of front. The philosophy behind the use

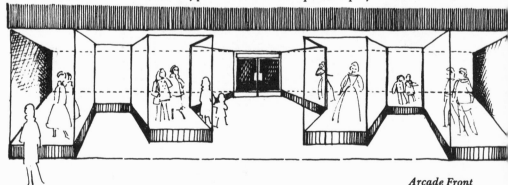

Arcade Front

of this front is a mass-merchandising one. In essence, there are only mannequins, merchandise, and price signs in the window, without benefit of props or backgrounds.

CLASSIFICATION OF WINDOW STYLES

A store may have any one of three major storefronts, with the straight front being the most predominant. Regardless of which type is used, the store still has a choice of window style. There are eight specific types: elevated, elevator, ramped, open-backed, corner, lobby, island, and shadow box.

THE ELEVATED WINDOW STYLE

As the straight storefront is the most common, so is the elevated window. This is a display window which is perpendicular to the sidewalk, flush with the building, and from twelve to eighteen inches above the level of the sidewalk. The window is raised as a safety precaution and to bring the merchandise closer to the customer's eye level. The floor of the window is parallel to the sidewalk and is usually carpeted in a neutral color. The depth and the height vary according to the physical structure of the building, but they are usually no less than six feet wide and ten feet high. The background and side panels, if there are any, are also of a neutral color. The window will have its own lighting system (usually track lighting). The only viewpoint for the customer is from the outside, and thus it presents a one-sided viewpoint.

Elevated Window

ELEVATOR WINDOWS

Elevator windows are an expensive addition to a store, with the only difference between them and an elevated window being the fact that the floor in an elevator window can be raised and

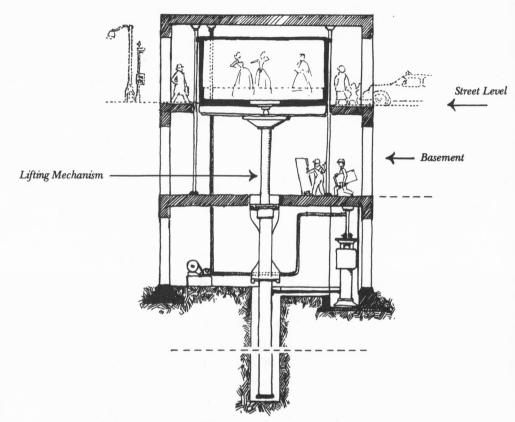

Street Level

Basement

Lifting Mechanism

lowered at will. The display department is located in the basement beneath the window. This facilitates the changing of the windows in that the floor is lowered, the old display is removed, the new one is installed, and the floor is raised back in place. Prestige stores in major cities will invest in this type of window.

RAMPED WINDOWS

Ramped windows are also a variation of the elevated window with the only difference being that the floor is slanted from a low point at the front of the window to the back to form an inclined plane.

Any elevated window can be transformed into a ramped window by the addition of a ramp. The advantage here is that

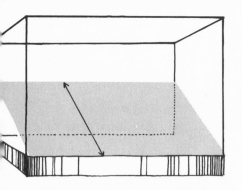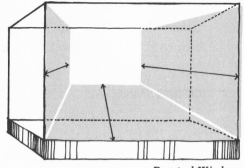

the merchandise in the back of the window will show up more clearly and will not be obstructed by the merchandise in the foreground. The same effect can be achieved by using a series of buildups.

OPEN-BACKED WINDOWS

Open-backed windows are, as the name implies, backless windows which permit the customer to see right into the store. They are usually an elevated window and give the effect of opening up the store to the customer. An open door is always more inviting than a closed one.

There are two problems associated with this type of window. First, the display must be constructed so as to be effective and not obstruct the view of the customer. The second is the loss of the storage space behind the window when the back is removed. *Cleanliness and maintenance become a much more important factor when open-backed windows are used.*

17

In summary, the merchandise presentation is in the front where the customer is attracted to it while being able to view into the store and see the merchandise assortment.

CORNER WINDOWS

Corner windows are the most important windows in the store. They are usually the largest windows in the store and are a focal point due to the convergence of two traffic patterns at the corner. The most important and the best merchandise should be scheduled for this window. The merchandise is viewable from two sides rather than just one as in an elevated window. Further effectiveness and maximum utilization of the window can be achieved through the installation of a revolving floor. Customers find corner windows interesting to watch because they can always tell what is current or spot a new trend by watching the merchandise featured here.

LOBBY AND ISLAND WINDOWS

Lobby and island windows are those found in an angled or arcade storefront, and they present the problems already mentioned. They are usually smaller than elevated windows and present limitations as to types of merchandise and props that can be effectively utilized in them.

Lobby and Island Windows

SHADOW-BOX WINDOWS

Shadow boxes are small windows which exist either alone or in part of a larger window. They create an effective display area for small, important merchandise such as jewelry. Good lighting is an essential factor for this type of window as it is totally enclosed. A larger window may be transformed into a shadow box for a dramatic effect by enclosing most of the window in a frame.

Knowing the physical properties of the different types of windows is basic. The important act of creation is the next step in the window-display process. However, most people are not aware of the intricacies involved in putting together a series of windows.

THE WINDOW CHANGE SCHEDULE

To maintain their effectiveness as sales tools, windows should be changed every ten days to two weeks, depending upon the merchandise and the season. The fashion or image windows, both in ready-to-wear and home furnishings, should be changed the most frequently to keep the newest trends constantly before the public. On that account *most large stores have a fashion co-ordinator in both areas who is responsible for a window schedule.*

A window schedule, issued monthly or every two months, presents the image and theme for each window and in some cases will list the specific merchandise to be displayed down to the last accessory for a dress. A theme is listed for each window which ties into the overall theme for the windows. They all tell a coordinated story. For example: a large Boston store has a series of four windows which present the fashion image for the home-furnishings division as well as eight other windows which feature current merchandise in home-furnishings-related fields.

The overall theme was GO NATURAL and in the four fashion windows it was stated: "GO NATURAL with wicker"; "GO NATURAL with redwood"; "GO NATURAL with rattan"; and "GO NATURAL with wrought iron." The overall theme was an extension of do-your-own-thing with summer furniture, but each window interpreted it in terms of a different customer and lifestyle.

The same type of story can also be told in the ready-to-wear windows. A series of windows can be captioned, "Colorful Chiffons Create Evening Splendor." This can be stated in four adjoining windows as well as any intervening shadow boxes.

Theme: "Colorful Chiffons"

THE ROLE OF THE DISPLAY DEPARTMENT

The window schedule is submitted to the display department, which has specific people assigned to do the windows. It is their function to physically interpret the ideas and themes presented. They must gather the appropriate merchandise, props, and accessories and create the merchandise presentations in the glass cases. Here is where their creativity and ability to improvise become the key to the success or failure of the finished product. It is common that in most stores you never have all the pieces to make a perfect puzzle. So, you borrow and create an illusion, which is to last only for the duration of the window.

INSTALLING A WINDOW

The window people also work on a schedule and can usually accomplish a series of windows (four) within a three-day period. The typical procedure followed for installing a home-furnishings fashion window involving a room setting would be as follows:

1   Review both the window schedule for theme and merchandise to be sold.
2   Formulate ideas for the display and review window layout drawn by display artist.
3   Scout the appropriate departments (gift shop, linens, china, crystals, silver, carpet, pictures, furniture) for the correct merchandise and accessories.
4   Check the display department for the appropriate props and fixtures if they are called for.
5   Sign out the appropriate merchandise in a merchandise requisition book.
7   Clean the floor and surrounding area in the window.
8   Install the new background for the display.
9   Arrange the furniture according to the layout.
10   Add accessories, props and fixtures.
11   Put in the sign.
12   Adjust the lighting.
13   Check the display from outside the window to assess the effect the customer will receive.
14   Return the old and unused merchandise promptly.

This is a simplified procedure that assumes that all the merchandise to be utilized is in the store. If not, prior arrangements must be made to have such items transferred.

Ready-to-wear windows are simpler to execute in that they do not involve as great a quantity and diversity of merchandise. However, the procedural steps are approximately the same in that the display artist plans, executes, and reviews each of his windows.

CLASSIFICATION OF WINDOW DISPLAYS

Windows may be classified by the types of merchandise used in them or by the purpose served by the windows. All windows obviously serve the purpose of enticing the customer to buy, whether it is done overtly or subtly. They also serve to educate the consuming public in what is new and hopefully in what is correct in style and taste.

INSTITUTIONAL WINDOW DISPLAYS

Most stores, depending upon their size, will run institutional windows throughout the year at special times.

An institutional display is not designed to promote store merchandise. It publicizes themes and events of public interest that are usually of a noncommercial nature.

Offering display space to such community interests is meant to generate goodwill between the store and its customers. This is a subtle but effective way of improving store patronage.

Larger stores found in major cities will have institutional windows at Christmastime which attract throngs of shoppers as well as sightseers. They are not selling anything but the image and public-spiritedness of the store itself. This classification of window becomes a tradition over a period of time, and customers expect it every year. The themes vary from year to year, but they are usually religious, civic, or fantasy oriented.

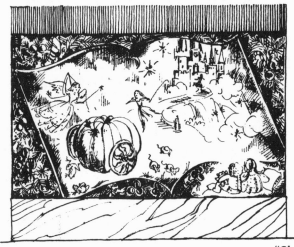

"Christmas"
Promotional Window

THE PROMOTIONAL WINDOW

Another classification of window display that serves a specific purpose is the promotional window. In essence, all windows are promotional in that they are selling something. However, a distinction exists in that promotional windows are used for SALE merchandise at specific times of the year. The twice-yearly white sale of the large department stores is an example of this type of *promotional window.* Discounters always have promotional windows, for they operate on a low margin - high turnover basis with their specially-priced merchandise as their main inventory.

Sales Promotion Window

Depending upon the image and price level of the store, promotional windows may or may not be utilized. Small, specialty chain stores declare their sales by filling the window with merchandise and big red "SALE" signs. Other stores will maintain the same format for their promotional windows as that of their regular and fashion windows. They will simply add a subtle sign announcing that there is a reduction in the price of their goods.

Sophisticated stores would never take the approach of a Casual Corner as it is not consistent with their image or their clientele.

THE FASHION WINDOWS

A large department store will have a certain number of windows in which the most fashionable merchandise is consistently presented. This applies to both ready-to-wear and home furnishings. This type of window is termed a *fashion window*. This window is geared more toward store image than to customer purchase. It lets the public know that the store is a front-runner in the areas of ready-to-wear and home furnishings and has the latest in both areas. The other windows of the store are also fashionable in their presentation and selection of the merchandise, but these windows are more concerned with actual sales than customer education. The fashion window first sells the concept, then the product.

Fashion windows are usually done as a coordinated grouping for the most effective impact.

Fashion Window

WINDOW-CLASSIFICATION SYSTEM

In each type of window, a merchandise classification system may be used. There are four window designations:

1. One-item window
2. Line-of-goods window
3. Related-merchandise window
4. Miscellaneous window

The one-item window is used to create a dramatic effect and might display an expensive fur coat or an exquisite piece of jewelry.

One Item Window Display

A line-of-goods window employs merchandise *all of the same classification.* Merchandise differences occur only in style, color, or design. A shirt shop could use such a window.

Line of Goods   Display

A related-merchandise window would be one in which all the merchandise relates to a story. It could be a color and usage relationship with all red, white, and blue merchandise for the bathroom environment. It could be a theme relationship between the merchandise; all the goods are potential Father's Day gifts.

Evening   Sports   Lingerie

"Rainbow Theme"

The miscellaneous window is one in which there is no apparent relationship between the items on an overall basis: a window in a "Five and Dime" would be an example of this classification.

Miscellaneous Window

ATTRACTIVENESS IS IMPORTANT

In each of these windows it is important that the merchandise be fresh, clean, and attractively arranged. As much care should be taken with a regular merchandise window as with a fashion presentation. The windows invite customers into the store, and they will expect continuity once inside. Coordination between the exterior displays and the interior displays is vital if the store is to present a unified image to the customer.

FOR REVIEW AND DISCUSSION

1. In terms of merchandising, describe how windows convey the store's character or image.
2. Explain why downtown stores tend to have more window space than suburban stores.
3. How do most discount stores utilize their window space?
4. When setting up a display for a straight-front type of window having a slightly recessed entrance or foyer, where would the most important merchandise be displayed? Why?
5. Why is an angled storefront more advantageous to a small, narrow store?
6. What advantages are gained by the use of elevated windows?
7. How does an elevator window create greater efficiency for a large department store?
8. Are there advantages in the use of ramped windows? Describe them.
9. Why do customers generally find corner windows important to watch?
10. How can a large window be converted for use as a shadow-box window?
11. What are some of the items that would be specified on a detailed window schedule?
12. Describe the role of the display department when it receives the window schedule.
13. What is the difference between an institutional window display and a promotional window display?
14. What kind of merchandise is generally found in a fashion window?
15. Name some of the items of merchandise that might be placed in a one-item window.

unit 3

Interior Display

Today's consumer is the most informed and aware consumer in our history. He or she is constantly bombarded with information from all media, and in some instances, the consumer will know the merchandise better than the salesperson. They are keenly attuned to what is new and to what should be available in the marketplace.

It is the job of the interior displays in a retail store to attract the attention of the consumers, register an idea, color, or item and induce them to purchase the merchandise.

The windows are effective merchandising tools in that they will initially bring the customer into the store. But, once inside, the interior displays must take over this function. The store interior should be an extension of the exterior theme in order to have maximum customer impact. A store cannot afford to present customers with two different personalities.

STORE LAYOUT

Each retail organization, be it a department store, specialty store, or discount house, is laid out in a manner suitable to its specific operation. Each has a number of locations within the store that are important from a display standpoint. An effective layout makes it easy for customers to buy and is efficient from the proprietor's point of view. Keep in mind that display considerations are inseparable from layout.

The type of floor plan used, whether gridiron or free-flow, will determine the different areas within the store to be used for display purposes, the type of fixturing selected, and the placement of the fixtures themselves.

THE GRIDIRON

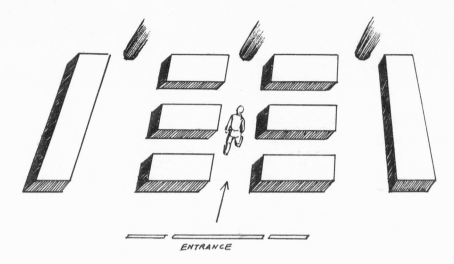

ENTRANCE

THE FREE FLOW

ENTRANCE

The gridiron plan is rigid, and due to its rather inflexible layout, the types of display opportunities are limited.

The free-flow plan is the one used most frequently in department stores and specialty shops.

Merchandise Island

The free-flow plan is much more flexible and permits the use of many different types of display areas within the interior of the store such as cases, platforms, shadow boxes, ledges, island areas, and environmental settings. A department or specialty store will use any or all of these depending upon its size and merchandise assortment.

DISPLAY AREAS

In the multistory store, the most valuable space is the main floor. The most valuable space on the main floor is between an entrance and an escalator or elevator. Here is where aisles, tables, gondolas, or island areas with pick-up merchandise are utilized. *Pick-up merchandise* is that which the customer is either looking for because of an advertised sale, or it is merchandise that is featured as an impulse item. The need for attractive controlled displays in this area is not paramount because of the heavy traffic volume. An orderly mass merchandise arrangement will move the merchandise just as quickly as an elaborate display.

The merchandise assortment is changed frequently, as is the classification.

DISPLAY CASES

The display areas of a large department store are various in nature, and their usage is determined primarily by the merchandise. Display cases serve a triple purpose. First, they act to form a selling area on the floor by physically enclosing space. Second, they serve for storage of merchandise since the goods can be stacked in the cases. Third, they are a display unit.

Display Case

Cases are rectangular boxes constructed of glass on the front, two sides, and the top. The back is usually enclosed with sliding doors. The front may be glass about two-thirds of the way to the floor or be partially enclosed with a wooden or synthetic front, as in jewelry cases. The lighting is from a fluorescent tube attached to the inside top of the case. The bottom of the case is a pad made from foam core which is covered with a material that relates to the trim of the particular season. For example, at Christmas the pad would be covered with red felt, or in the spring it would be covered with a green fern pattern.

If the case is large enough, the back and the sides will also be covered. This material, be it felt, silk moire, or cotton, will determine the mood of the case and should be appropriate in color and feel for the merchandise being displayed. Small props such as swags of Christmas garland or small greenery can be added for interest. Buildups such as cork blocks or fabric-covered boxes are used to vary the levels of the merchandise.

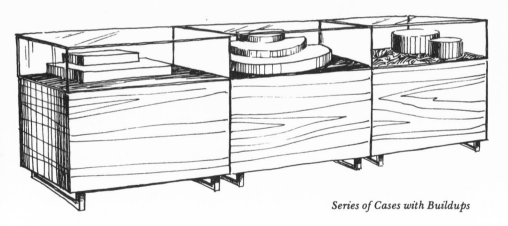

Series of Cases with Buildups

The most important considerations when doing a case are the scale of the merchandise and the props and the viewpoint of the customer. Most merchandise is seen from above with the customer looking down through the case; this is especially true in jewelry and cosmetic cases. Cases should be simple and uncluttered and *as in all displays, the merchandise should be dominant and not the display props.* A series of cases will form a counter and should present a coordinated story to the customer. Customer impact should occur when they view a series of cases.

PLATFORMS

Platforms are used to distinguish a display from the normal floor of a department store. They are usually six to eight inches in height and come in various sizes with the most common being four by eight feet. They are either rectangular or round in design and are available commercially. They may also be constructed by the display department from wood and then covered with a suitable material. The commercial models are available with a tile or a wood-parquet top.

Platform →

Platforms are used to highlight merchandise in different areas of the store. Mannequins are positioned on them in the ready-to-wear department with basic props either on the platform or suspended behind it. Platforms are very important in the home-furnishings department of a store, for they are used to build vignettes. These are small versions of what a manufacturer's showroom would look like or a display giving a total look through related merchandise such as a bath-shop vignette.

← *Platform*

Bath Vignette

34

INTERIOR SHADOW-BOXES

Shadow boxes within the store are similar in nature to the ones used as windows. Inside the store they are usually located behind counters, especially in the jewelry department. They are trimmed to reflect the season and should show the merchandise so that it dominates. The lighting is from concealed fluorescent tubes or spotlights in the top of the shadow-box.

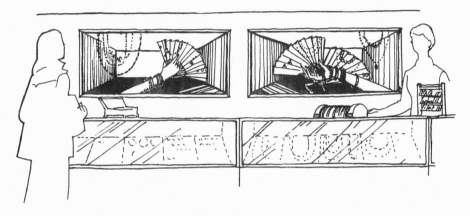

LEDGES

Ledges are found in two areas of the store and are used in a different manner than other areas. One type of ledge is recessed into the wall above a set of shelves. Here a display may be done showing the merchandise stored below it or merchandise from the entire department. The lighting is fluorescent and usually not efficient. The addition of props is necessary for this type of display to work. The space is difficult to work with in that the width-to-length proportion is very distorted.

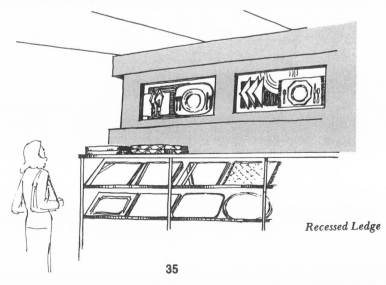

Recessed Ledge

The other area termed a ledge is the area which is the top of the center unit in a selling area. It is here that the main portion of the seasonal trim is situated. Palm trees for cruise time, Christmas trees at Christmas, plants and terrariums at springtime will all be situated on the ledges. This is because they are open spaces which would be extremely difficult to use for merchandise presentation. They are more effective for image presentations. The major problem with a ledge of this type is that it is visible from all four sides and the display must be designed accordingly.

Ledge Display

ISLAND AREAS

Island areas are similar to platforms except that they are stationary and are planned in the preliminary layout of the store. They are located in all parts of the store but especially near escalators, elevators, the entrances to important shops, and other high-traffic areas. *Permanent lighting fixtures, spotlights, have been installed above these areas for maximum lighting effect.* The platforms themselves are finished to coordinate with the general decor of the store, and different moods are achieved through the manipulation of backgrounds and props. As with cases, platforms, and ledges, the island areas relate to the seasonal trim and theme.

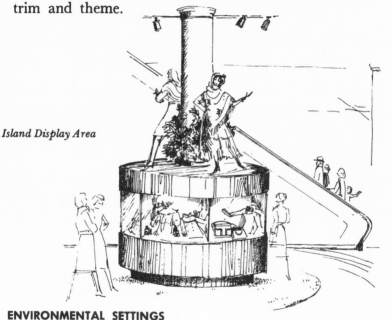

Island Display Area

ENVIRONMENTAL SETTINGS

Environmental settings are exclusive to a department store or specialty store which has a furniture and home-furnishings division. *An environmental setting is a simulated room setting complete with furniture, carpeting, and all appropriate accessories* which is installed in a three-walled "room" which has an appropriate wall covering on the wall. This type of display allows the customer the opportunity of seeing exactly how a group of furniture will look in a simulated room environment. From a display standpoint it is very challenging, in that it forces the display person to work·on a large scale and with the whole environment, not just a part.

Environmental Settings

Living rooms, bedrooms, dining rooms, family rooms, and children's rooms are all represented. Lamps, pictures, bedspreads and the total accessories picture are the merchandise that have to be worked with and brought to life. Environmental room settings are designed by the Home Furnishings Coordinator and are then assembled and maintained by the display department.

COORDINATION OF DISPLAYS AND THEMES

The windows and the interior of the store must be considered as one in terms of coordination. Each season has a specific trim which is registered in each department throughout the store and in the windows. When it is Christmas the customer knows it is Christmas from seeing the trees in the window, the garland in the corset department. This total coordination is true not only for seasonal displays, but also for magazine tie-ins and special promotions.

Certain large stores can become *House and Garden* stores which means that they receive editorial credits in the magazine, often relating to the color trends put forth by the magazine. For example, the *House & Garden* color and promotional theme might be "Sunshine Yellows." The store would then be bathed in yellows from the creamiest apricot to the most vibrant sun-yellow. This color story would be reflected in the windows, in the interior displays, and in the merchandise in every department. All the displays, both exterior and interior, would be keyed to yellow, with white, green, and orange used as accents. The customer is overwhelmed with the registration of yellow in everything from pillows to sheets to rugs. A further coordination could be accomplished through the use of signs bearing the "Sunshine Yellow" logo.

SPECIAL PROMOTIONS

Special promotions are treated the same way in that all departments are involved from a merchandise and display standpoint. A special promotion may be one brought in by the store using outside resources and people, or it may be self-generated. using specific store merchandise.

Another promotion could be entitled "Strawberry Treat." All interior displays in the "Store for Homes" would be built around this theme. The merchandise is all either strawberry patterned or in the color family of red with accents of green and white. The windows would reflect the same theme. Signs and the use of a large commercially-made three-dimensional strawberry would tie the whole promotion together.

"Strawberry Treat"
Promotional Theme

Whether it is a series of windows, cases, a room setting, or a special promotion, the key to a successful display is coordination and a unified presentation. There must not only be continuity in the individual displays but also in the store as a whole. The exterior must reflect the interior and the interior must reflect the exterior. If this is accomplished, the image of the store as well as its character will be projected and registered with the customer.

FOR REVIEW AND DISCUSSION

1. Why is the gridiron store plan considered to be rigid in terms of visual merchandising or display opportunities?
2. What is pick-up merchandise, and where is it generally positioned in the store?
3. How would you trim a display case in preparation for the Christmas season?
4. How are platforms used in a display situation?
5. Where in the store are island areas generally situated?
6. What types of stores primarily use environmental display settings?
7. What is a house-and-garden store?

unit 4

The Materials
of Visual Merchandising

Display or visual merchandising is essentially the art of illusion, the art of endowing merchandise with a salable quality whether it is inherent in the merchandise or not. The merchandise is not all that the display artist has to work with. In his bag of tricks he has various fixtures, innumerable props, and endless materials from which to create the fantasies and dramatic effects which the customer has come to expect. As in the world of the theater, what goes on backstage is crucial to the final production.

FIXTURES

Fixtures lend life and interest to merchandise and allow it to be shown in a new perspective to the customer. The category of fixtures is broad and includes such items as stands, millinery heads, and forms. The size of the store and the display budget will be the determinant as to how many of these items will be available to the display artists.

THE STAND

The primary function of a stand is to add height to a display and enhance the appearance of the merchandise. They are usually found on the top of a counter, case, round, or gondola. Metal is the most common material for a stand, but they are also constructed from plastic. The metal stand has an adjustable rod which allows it to increase in height to accommodate different sizes of merchandise.

The base of the stand is standard, while various attachments screw onto the top of it to accommodate assorted classifications of merchandise. This flexibility makes stands one of the most important fixtures that the display artist has to work with.

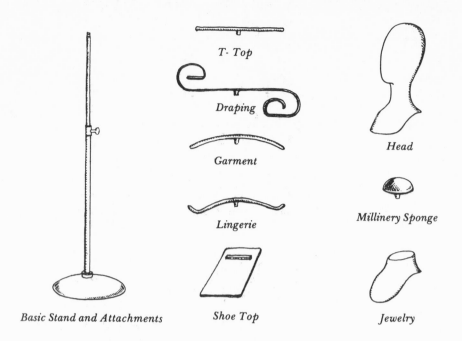

T- Top

Draping

Garment

Lingerie

Shoe Top

Head

Millinery Sponge

Jewelry

Basic Stand and Attachments

The most basic of the tops is the T-top which is a straight bar perpendicular to the stand over which loose, flowing items such as scarves are draped.

A stand is particularly effective for the display of sleeveless lingerie when the proper stand top is utilized. Lingerie tops for stands were especially developed to curve as human shoulders and thereby create a semblance of human character when the stand is adjusted to the proper height. The ends of lingerie tops turn upward so that the slim straps of slips and gowns will not slide off the bar.

Garment tops also curve as human shoulders which will approximate human form. Since they are used to display garments having sleeves, the ends of the garment top do not turn up.

THE SHIRT TOP

In the men's area the most common top is the shirt top which is of two types: *metal* and *balsa wood*. The *metal top* is a plate with an upturned lip on the bottom which allows a packaged shirt to be displayed at an angle to the customer's viewpoint. A tie may be added to create a total look.

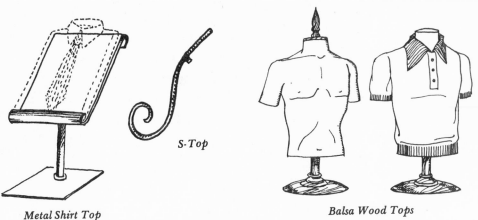

Metal Shirt Top   *S-Top*   *Balsa Wood Tops*

A variation of this top is an *S-top* which is a metal bar curved into the shape of an S into which the shirt is slipped. This does not present as crisp an appearance as the other top.

The *balsa wood top* offers more life to the merchandise in that the shirt is taken out of its protective wrapper, unpinned, and then repinned to the balsa wood top with the excess of the shirt either tucked under the top or folded into layers at the bottom of the shirt top. The sleeves of the shirt are ruffled or puffed up to add character and individuality to the display. A tie may also be added to give a finished look as well as to show merchandise coordination. Both of these tops have flexible adjustments at the point of attachment to the stand so the merchandise may be angled toward the customer.

THE SHOE TOP

In the shoe department one will find a top termed a *shoe top*. This is one of two types. The first is a metal plate with two wedges near the top which hold the heel of the shoe in place

Metal Shoe Top

Plastic Shoe Top

and prevent slippage. The other is a plastic unit which is curved at the end to hold the shoe in place. They both may be for either a single shoe or a pair of shoes. An effective shoe display can be created by using a number of stands with shoe tops all adjusted to varying heights so each shoe stands on its own merit as well as creating an interesting shoe story.

MILLINERY AND WIG FIXTURES

In the millinery and wig departments there are several types of fixtures. There are stands which have millinery sponges attached to the top of them. There are also multi-arm stands which have permanent sponge tops. And there are fixtures classified as heads. These are all used to display millinery and wigs. The heads are made of either rubber, plastic, or styrofoam. They may be either realistic in representation or imaginary in design. Buildups are needed underneath the heads to give them height and to create visual interest in this type of display.

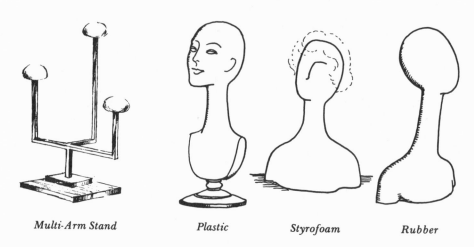

Multi-Arm Stand   *Plastic*   *Styrofoam*   *Rubber*

FORMS

In all of the ready-to-wear departments in a store, one will find display fixtures referred to as forms, which include full and partial bodies of both male and female figures. There are full-scale mannequins, torsos, hands, arms, and legs, all used for specific merchandise and purposes.

MANNEQUINS

Mannequins are full-figure forms of men, women, and children constructed out of various materials. Early mannequins were made from wax. Later they were molded in plaster or papier-maché. Still later, rubber was used. Modern mannequins are made from high-impact plastic and fiberglass. Fiberglass figures are 10 to 12 pounds lighter than older models. Other types were modeled after the formal, remote and "stiff" Victorian ideal of womanhood. Today's mannequins reflect the animated, informal and friendly mood of the times. A modern mannequin will have real eyelashes, a lifelike wig, and will relate in body shape to the clothes that she is wearing.

Victorian Mannequin

During the '40's, mannequins looked like sturdy athletes in order to fit the tailored look of the decade; they had broad shoulders and slim hips. The fifties' models best displayed the flat-chested, full-petticoat styles and were modeled with bigger hips.

There was a slimming down of the mannequins of the 1960's and an introduction of more action into their poses. A change in the fashions had caused a change in the physical appearance of the mannequins.

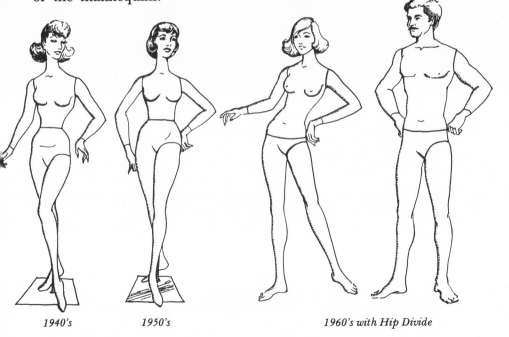

1940's   1950's   1960's with Hip Divide

At this point, mannequins became more animated in appearance, and they have taken on a sculptured effect. Neck bones are observable as are dimples in the knees. They are divided at the hip so that there won't be a line showing when they're dressed in bikinis.

This sculpturing of the mannequin has given them a more realistic, natural appearance, to the point that children occasionally mistake the mannequins for real people.

FUTURISTIC MANNEQUINS

Mannequins are also made in futuristic versions with no facial expressions or realistic appearance save for the contours of the facial structure and body. These are made from fiberglass and are a color other than flesh, usually off-white or silver. *This type of mannequin is limited in its use due to its extreme appearance and usually extreme pose.* The futuristic mannequin is effectively utilized in a girl's junior department or small boutique where realism is not important and where only one or two mannequins are required.

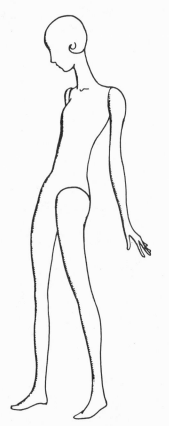

Futuristic Mannequin

MALE MANNEQUINS

The male mannequins have also been updated away from the Tarzan image. They are no longer staid and somber in appearance. Now they are slimmer, have more expression, longer hair, and mustaches appear on many.

PARTIAL MANNEQUINS

In the initial blueprint for mannequins for a store, the display director must also plan for torso forms and partial forms such as hands and legs. These last two are found less in stores today, but are still used as display fixtures.

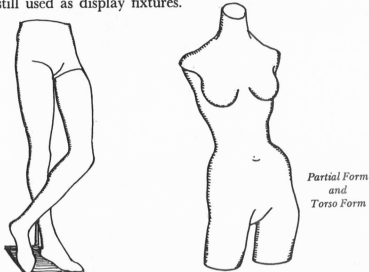

Partial Form and Torso Form

Torsos are found mainly in the men's department where they are used to show suits, sport coats, outerwear, underwear, shirts, and sweaters. They are forms which represent the area of the male body from the neck to the pelvis without arms or head and are made from rubber or a cloth-covered heavy cardboard. The rubber ones are more difficult to work with in that pins do not readily go into them. The other type is easier to work with. They both may either be on a stand or free-standing. A complete outfit of a sport coat, shirt, and tie may be shown on a torso. Again the trick of pinning is utilized to insure a crisp appearance.

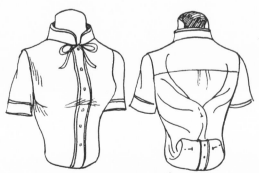

Illustration of Pinning

47

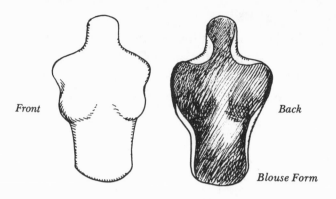

Front   *Back*

Blouse Form

Blouse forms are similar in principle to a torso , but they are smaller and represent the area of the female body from the neck to the waist. They are usually placed on a counter rather than a platform. They are not solid as is the torso and they are made from molded plastic.

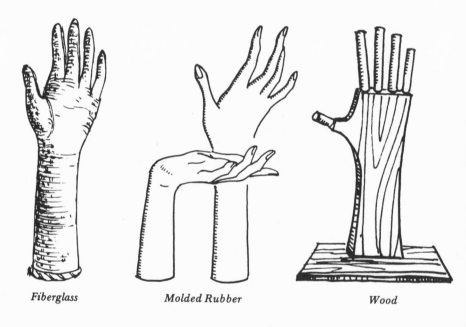

Fiberglass   *Molded Rubber*   *Wood*

Hands are still used in glove departments and they vary tremendously. There is the traditional molded-rubber or plastic hand and those made out of wood and fiberglass which are interpretive rather than realistic in appearance. They also appear in jewelry departments to show off particular items.

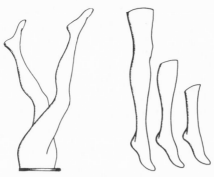

Leg Forms

Legs are found in a hosiery department and are used in displays in the cases to show the new styles and colors of hosiery. Traditional materials have been replaced with newer and more innovative materials such as styrofoam and foam core, which are lighter, easier to work with, and more flexible for creative displays than molded-rubber legs.

Mannequins, torsos, and appendages are all extremely important fixtures in any ready-to-wear area, for these are the vehicles which present the merchandise to the public in the most attractive and understandable manner. Each item stands on its own merit as well as being a part of the whole.

There are also fixtures in a store which permit the merchandise to be shown in the open where the customer can inspect and select it without the help of a salesperson. These self-service fixtures are gondolas, tables, rounds, A-frames, and T-stands. These more appropriately come under the jurisdiction of the store planning department, but it is part of the job of the display department to revitalize selling departments and to create new departments by manipulating the position of these fixtures.

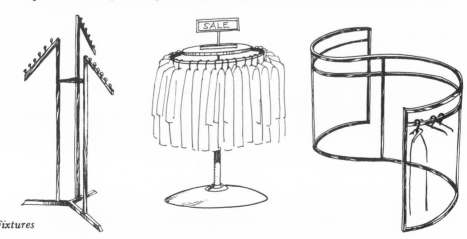

n Fixtures

MANNEQUIN COSTS

All mannequins are an expensive initial investment for a store. When a store is laid out, the display director will key each area for the number and type of mannequins required and draw up a budget for them. *This initial purchase of mannequins and forms will last for about two years, when refurbishing and replacement should begin.*

CLEANING

Mannequins can be cleaned with an industrial cleaner to keep them fresh in appearance. They can be sent out for an overhaul which will increase their store life. Because of their high cost and relative fragility, they are one fixture that requires constant maintenance and care.

DETERIORATION

After about a year of use in the main window, a mannequin may be shifted to small side windows, then to interior displays. With use, handling, and exposure to sun and display lights, mannequins deteriorate. They must be refinished periodically and given new hair styles.

DRESSING A MANNEQUIN

Customers are always fascinated when they stop to watch a window or an in-store display being changed, especially when it comes to changing the mannequin. Being able to dress a mannequin is an art in itself. Most mannequins split into two portions at either the waistline or the hipline, and the appendages all come off.

PROCEDURE

The steps one should follow in putting a complete outfit on a Size 8 female mannequin are as follows:

1. Remove the old outfit and completely disassemble the mannequin, laying all the parts on the floor. Put the right members to the right and the left members to the left.

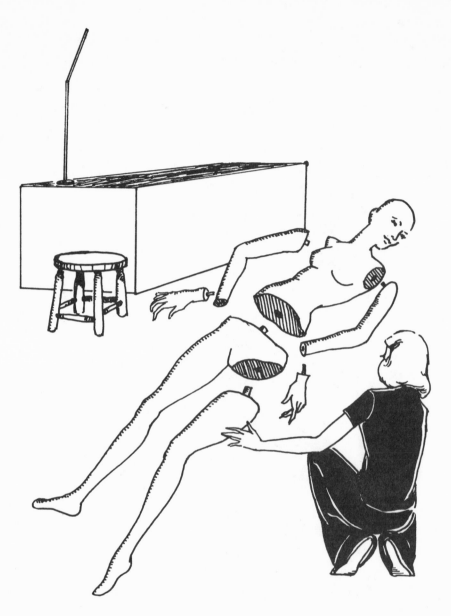

Mannequin disassembled with members on right and left.

2. Start with the bottom portion of the mannequin. Put a pair of pantyhose on the lower portion. (Note: A display department should have a selection of pantyhose in different colors so as not to book out a new pair every time a mannequin change is made.)

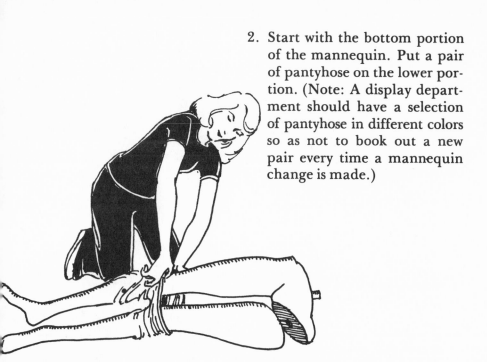

3. Put on the skirt.

4. Put the shoes on. If it is an older mannequin it will have a stand, so position the bottom portion on the stand by inserting the vertical metal rod into the·aperture in the lower portion. If it is a newer mannequin, it will be free-standing.

5. Position the upper portion on the lower portion.

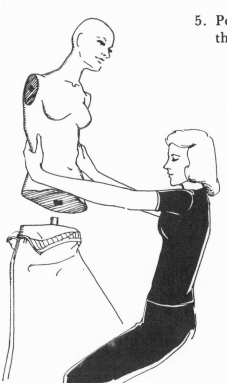

6. Put the blouse on by inserting the action arm in the sleeve and locking it into the top. Put the static arm into the other sleeve and lock it in.

7. Button the blouse and tuck it into the skirt. Pull the blouse from the front to back so that it fits correctly and does not gap.

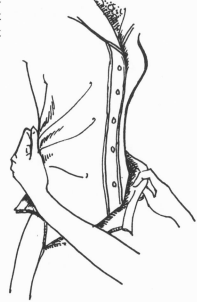

8. Put the hands on the wrists, first adding any wrist jewelry which will not fit over the hands.

9. Put on the head and position the wig on the head. The hair style of the wig should correspond to the style and feel of the outfit. Add any neck jewelry.

10. Add a handbag either on the wrist or over the shoulder.

11. The mannequin is ready for positioning in the window or display. The last step is to position the lighting and inspect it from the viewpoint of the customer.

The same basic steps may be followed for any type of mannequin and for any type of outfit. Each mannequin is distinct in that no two will fit together in exactly the same manner, and the easiest way to learn to dress a mannequin is through experience.

MANNEQUIN SIZES

Mannequins come in sizes which correspond to ready-to-wear sizes, and the appropriate-size merchandise should be used on the appropriate-size mannequins. This is not always possible especially with the more expensive merchandise, such as designer clothes, so that pinning may be necessary. *Pinning is the procedure of altering a garment, without physically changing it,* so that it appears to fit the mannequin. *This can only be done in displays where the customer and the public cannot see the backs of the mannequins,* for this is where the pinning is done. This is commonly used in advertising photography.

Whether it is pinned together or the correct size, the merchandise should be clean, new, and freshly pressed before going on the mannequin. Once on the mannequin, it is the responsibility of the display artist to see that it fits correctly and hangs properly. Each mannequin should look like he or she stepped out of the proverbial bandbox.

PROPS

In addition to the basic fixtures already mentioned, the display artist has at his disposal a classification known as props. These are the items that lend the creative spark, the individual touch, the store signature to a display. They may be purchased commercially, made in the store, or pulled from yesterday's trash. Any unusual or everyday object or discard can, with ingenuity, be turned into a display prop. Basically, anything has the potential for becoming a display prop; it is what the display artist sees in it, whether color, shape, or texture, that will determine its eventual use. The unusual nature or unexpectedness of a prop will cause customer comment. Junkyard finds of abandoned machinery placed in a display window could make a customer wonder "what is it?" and enter the store to ask.

Props are an important component of any display, but they are especially valuable for ready-to-wear. Displays in the home-furnishings area such as domestics, housewares, and gifts depend heavily on the props to pull the display together. For example, a display of clocks would not mean much by itself, but add some *natural-wood crates* in various sizes, some greenery, and you are telling a natural story. In ready-to-wear, props also serve to enhance the display.

They may be used to create a mood and environment for a window display — even a corner bridal window. The bridal gown and the attendant's gown could be given a country feeling through a careful selection of materials and colorations. to them through a careful selection of materials and colorations. The story would really come alive with the addition of props of a barnyard complete with hay, a cow, sheep, and the like.

SOURCES OF PROPS

There are a multitude of display houses which supply props, trims and various materials to retail stores. With these materials it is possible for the inventive display department to create its own props at a much lower cost.

The only caution about props is that at times customers will become irate if they cannot purchase a certain prop they see in a display. This is especially true when antiques are used. It is advisable to tag everything "PROPERTY OF THE DISPLAY DEPARTMENT" and alert salespeople to the fact. Some display houses will sell to the public, and a customer will always appreciate being told where to purchase an item rather than being told that it is not available.

MATERIALS OF DISPLAY

The materials that a display department has at its disposal are as limitless as its imagination and its budget. Two of the basics for any department, no matter how large or small, are various fabrics and felt. The pattern and the color will depend upon the season and the merchandise; green fern print for spring; red/brown/green patchwork for fall; red/green geometric for Christmas.

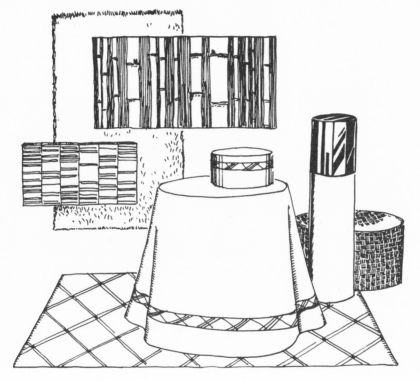

Fabrics in Use

FABRIC

Fabric is used for covering pads which are used in cases and on tables; for tablecloths; for covering cubes to be used in buildups; and as backgrounds.

FELT

Felt is used in much the same manner and will also color-coordinate with the season. Fabric and felt are easy to work with since they can be stretched taut and will look crisp in appearance.

NO-SEAM PAPER

No-seam paper is the mainstay for the backgrounds in the window. This is, as the name implies, durable heavyweight paper which comes in a roll nine feet in width and of various lengths. It is made in all colors of the rainbow, and the advantage of it is that it will cover the background of a window without any seaming. Usually it is lightly stapled at each side of the back, and the remaining paper is allowed to curl so as to give the appearance of having a slender column on each side of the window.

No-Seam Paper Installed

SPRAY PAINT

Spray paint is another staple item in the display cupboard. The colors are multiple as are the functions. The easiest, quickest, and cheapest way to change the appearance of a prop is to paint it.

STYRENE FOAM CORES

Little that is done in display is permanent, so a lightweight multi-purpose material is needed. Foam Core is a trade name for a board that consists of a sandwich of porous polystyrene foam covered on both sides with white clay paper. It is manufactured in four-foot-by-eight-foot sheets and can be cut with a

mat knife. The uses for it are endless. It is used for the pads in the cases or for any background that has to be covered with fabric. Figures, both human and animal, may be cut from it and then spray painted. Whole display fixtures such as a castle for a toy department can be constructed with Foam Core. It is also good in that most mediums will adhere to its surface.

STYROFOAM

Styrofoam can be put to good use in many areas due to its lightness and ability to be cut with either a mat knife or a saw. Much of the lettering that is used to identify shops or certain areas within a store is made of styrofoam and then painted with

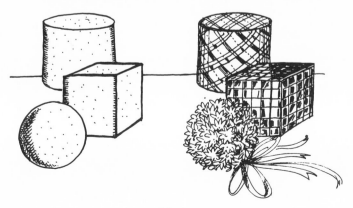

spray paint. Styrofoam is also good for buildups in a display and can be covered with fabric or felt. This material is useful because of its ability to have merchandise inserted into it. For this reason it makes an excellent base for displays where merchandise, such as silverware, must stand upright to be seen properly.

TOOLS

The other materials which the display artist uses frequently are those which would be found in any well-stocked toolbox. In fact, display artists use a toolbox to transport their tools of the trade. They include these basic items:

1. Hanson staple gun
2. Spray adhesive
3. Double-face tape
4. Masking tape
5. Different gauges of wire
6. Assorted nails and screws
7. Ruler
8. Mat knife
9. Assorted carpenter's tools (hammer, saw, etc.)

These are all necessary for carrying on day-to-day duties. For more elaborate construction there is a carpenter shop equipped to handle larger projects.

For the display artist to competently carry out the task of enticing the consumers into the large department store and then to convince them to buy, all of the aforementioned fixtures, props, and materials must be available. However, as a store decreases in size, so will its display budget and the number of display materials. Regardless of size, display is as important in a small boutique as it is in a large department store. The display artist must keep abreast of the latest developments in materials and acquire them as his budget allows. Effective displays are created from innate talent and creativity as well as proper and adequate props, fixtures, and merchandise.

FOR REVIEW AND DISCUSSION

1. Can you support the idea that visual merchandising is essentially the art of illusion?
2. What do you feel is the most important display fixture that the display artist has to work with? Why?
3. Mannequins used in the main windows of the store tend to fall into disrepair after about a year. How can additional use be gotten from such mannequins?
4. Can you name the steps and procedure for putting a complete outfit on a female mannequin?
5. In setting up a merchandise display, what function is served by props?
6. Where can props be found?
7. What is "Foam Core"?
8. How many uses can you think of for styrofoam in setting up merchandise displays?

unit 5

The Components
Of Visual Merchandising

Visual Merchandising is an art form in that it follows the same basic principles and elements of design that are employed in all recognized art forms. The main difference is that Visual Merchandising creations are temporary in nature and are created for a merchandising purpose rather than a purely aesthetic one. However, to be successful and accomplish their primary purpose of selling, the displays must be constructed according to the rules of good design. The presentation of the merchandise rather than the quantity of merchandise displayed will determine eventual sales.

Display artists have the merchandise, fixtures, props, and materials at their disposal to create various types of exhibits. It is these tangible objects which they must combine with the intangible components of visual merchandising. They must know how to use the various display formats, the principles and elements of visual merchandising, lighting, and color to achieve the maximum effect in each presentation. For it is the totality of the display that is important if a message is to be presented to and registered with the customer.

The success of any display can be measured in two ways:
1. By the resulting sales
2. By the artistic merit of the display itself

DISPLAY FORMATS

The format of the display must be consistent with the merchandise and the area in which the display is being set up. There are a number of formats in use today, with the three most common being *the step format, the pyramid format,* and *the zigzag format.* These can be used with almost any classification of merchandise and can be used in any type of display.

THE STEP FORMAT

The step format is a gradation in levels from lowest to highest with all the levels being parallel. If looked at from the side, the display would approximate a series of steps. There are commercially-constructed risers which may be utilized in this type of format or the steps may be constructed from wooden boards,

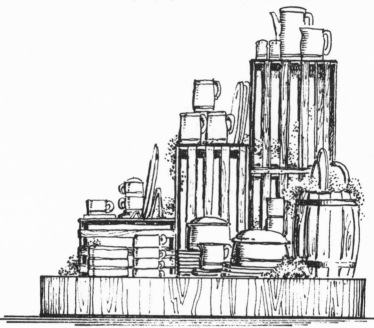

homosite, concrete blocks, or anything that lends itself to this type of display. Items such as old fruit crates and felt-covered boards create the correct feeling and provide a step format shown in the illustration. With this format the display may be either symmetrically or asymmetrically balanced, depending upon the impact desired and the merchandise used.

The eye movement in this type of display is upward and to the back because of the configuration of the steps.

THE PYRAMID FORMAT

The pyramid format approximates the shape of a three-sided figure. If the top of the form is used as the apex and a line is drawn down to the right to the luggage and down to the left to the luggage, one will recognize the pyramid shape. Whether the pyramid is in a horizontal or vertical position, the merchandise at the base of the pyramid will be larger and more spread-out and the items will be smaller and more compact as they near the top. This format is especially effective when the merchandise is all the same shape, such as boxes in a supermarket.

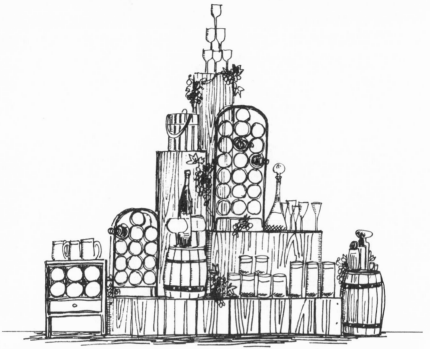

Pyramid Format

The balance used with this format is usually symmetrical due to the format itself, but it is possible to use informal balance if done correctly. The eye movement here would also be from the bottom upward. The eye is led to the pinnacle through the lines of the merchandise. The pyramid format is more static than the step arangement.

THE ZIGZAG FORMAT

A combination of both the step format and the pyramid format is the zigzag format. This type of display is alive, has a lot of movement within it, and moves the eye because of various heights in the display.

The merchandise is usually arranged in steps designed to move the customer's eye from lower right to upper left. The steps are not uniform in height, and this increases the areas in the display that can be used as focal points. The balance used in a zigzag display is always asymmetrical due to the various levels of merchandise. *This format is especially effective where there are a large number of items to be shown.*

Zig-Zag Format

ELEMENTS OF VISUAL EFFECT

Within the different formats used for displays there are certain elements of visual merchandising which must be adhered to if the display is to work. These elements encompass line, shape, size, texture, color, and weight and have an ability to bring life to the merchandise and to create mood, movement, and direction in a display.

LINE

The lines in a display come from the merchandise itself as well as from the positioning of the merchandise, and they impart specific meaning to the customer. A line may be either straight or curved with different direction to it.

The straight line produces a feeling of precision, rigidity, directness. *The curved line* gives the feeling of flexibility, action, and a flowing continuity. *The horizontal line* represents calm, quiet, and restfulness. It may also give the impression of width.

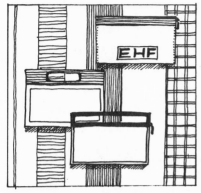

Straight Line Display

Curved Line Display

Horizontal Display

Vertical Display

The vertical line implies poise, balance, dignity, and height. *A diagonal line* can create different reactions. Usually a diagonal from high left to low right gives a feeling of action, leading the eye from the top left to the bottom right. It is exciting and indicates something is happening. A diagonal line from right (high) to left (low) will often convey a feeling of instability. It leads the eye through an unnatural movement and may produce a feeling of lack of confidence.

Diagonal Line Display

Lines join together to form two- and three-dimensional shapes which may be of any geometric configuration. The most common shapes utilized in visual merchandising are squares, circles, rectangles, triangles, cubes, spheres, boxes, and pyramids. All display areas are specific shapes. Windows are regular polygons as are cases. The shape of each display is determined by the outside boundaries of the display, whether it is free-standing or enclosed. The differing shapes of the merchandise have importance in their relationship with each other and to the total display.

A rectangular shape is more interesting than a square because of the relationship between the width and the length, or the two-to-three ratio.

The circle is considered to be "nature's beauty line" because it duplicates the sun and the full moon.

The shape of each object in the display is important because of the size associated with it. Size relates to the proportion in the display.

TEXTURE

The element of texture refers to the look or feel of an object's surface. Texture may be real or artificial. Texture is vital in a display, for it creates either harmony or contrast in the finished product. Real texture is inherent in the merchandise itself, such as the shine of silver or the slub in a silk material. The customer can actually feel this surface interest.

Texture

Artificial texture is created through different techniques and simulations so that a floor might look like cobblestone but in reality be smooth. They are optical illusions. Texture is important in environmental room settings to provide contrast and interest. Texture can also contribute to the weight of an object.

WEIGHT

Every piece of merchandise has an actual weight and an optical weight. For example, a foam pillow covered with dark fur may look heavy due to the texture and color but, in reality,

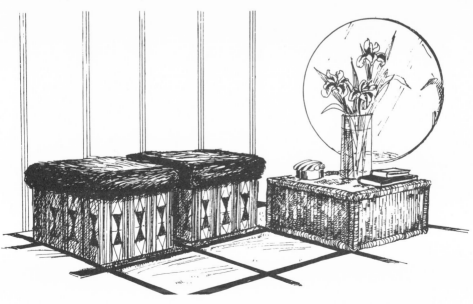

is very light due to the materials. *The optical weight is the more important in terms of visual merchandising and balance in a display.* The shape, color, and texture will determine the optical weight of an object, and this will determine its placement in the display. Lighting can also affect the optical weight of an object and may be used as a compensating factor.

PRINCIPLES OF VISUAL-MERCHANDISING DESIGN

The elements of visual-merchandising design relate to the objects being used in the display. The objects then have to be worked into the display according to the principles of visual merchandising design which are *balance, repetition, dominance, proportion, and contrast.* If all of these work in conjunction with one another, then harmony will be achieved in the display.

BALANCE

The optical weight of an object is of prime consideration when approaching the question of balance in a display. The display artist has a choice of either symmetrical or asymmetrical balance. *Symmetrical or formal balance* is more static and precise than asymmetrical or informal balance. It is more restrictive. In either case, the display is divided in half by an

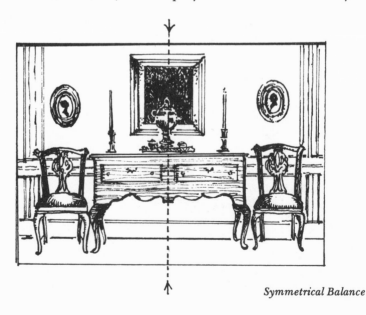

Symmetrical Balance

imaginary line which serves as a central axis. For formal balance, every object on the left-hand side of the line must be repeated on the right-hand side of the line. It is a simple balance scheme to use in that one side repeats the other.

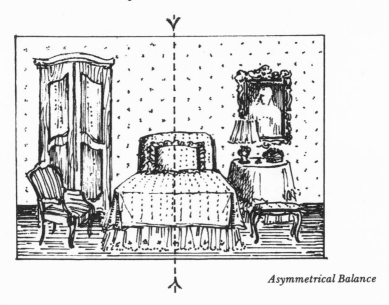

Asymmetrical Balance

Informal balance also operates with the imaginary central axis, but the items on each side do not repeat each other . . . the shapes and spaces repeat each other. If a line is drawn down the center of the bed, the shapes and spaces occupied by the armoire and the chair are repeated by those occupied by the picture, table, and bench. See illustration.

REPETITION

The principle of repetition creates continuity in a display. Repetition is the regular occurrence of an object or element throughout a display. Repetition may be accomplished through the use of color such as variations of red; the reappearance of a design element such as a strawberry; the use of similar shapes such as strawberry baskets and fruit boxes; the use of one texture such as china; or anything else that repeats itself in a display.

Repetition

Repetition may also be accomplished through the use of the same background in a series of windows. Repetition is important, for it registers the merchandise or the theme with the customer through visual impact.

Same Background

PROPORTION

Proportion and balance are both vital to a successful display, yet they are not synonymous. Proportion refers to what is usually accepted as being a proper relationship between objects and spaces. Proportion must be applied to the relationship between one object and another as well as the object and the whole. Items can purposely be made out of proportion for their normal context to create a certain impact. This exaggeration is evident in the accompanying illustration. The large strawberry is out of proportion for the small strawberry baskets, but it is used as the identifying motif in a coordinated series of displays. It is used for visual impact and theme identification.

Oversize Strawberry used for Visual Impact

CONTRAST

Contrast is a principle of visual-merchandising design which must be used carefully and skillfully. The contrast may come

between any one of the elements of visual merchandising design or created between the props and the merchandise. It is used as an attention-getter as illustrated here. There is no correlation between a tennis racket, tennis balls, and expensive gold jewelry except that they all are used by a man. The props attract the customer's attention, and the merchandise is specialized enough so that it will sell itself. Contrast should never be over used for it should always be able to take the unsuspecting customer by surprise.

DOMINANCE

Dominance is another term for focal point which every display should have to be entirely successful. This is the place in the display, the main area, to which the customer's eye is drawn. This can be accomplished through the use of color, unusual placement of merchandise, manipulation of line and eye movement, or lighting.

LIGHTING

Proper lighting is essential to a store for several reasons. The most important is that the customer must see the merchandise. The majority of the lighting in a store will be from fluorescent tubes because it looks more like daylight than incandescent lighting. It gives off less glare and is cooler. The long fluorescent tubes are easily installed in cases and ceilings. The tubes last longer than incandescent and give off far more light for the amount of electricity consumed.

Fluorescent Lighting

For concentrated lighting on specific parts of a display, spotlights will be used with one-hundred to three-hundred-watt bulbs. These act to highlight merchandise in a display or act as mood lighting. The main problem with spotlights is their intense heat.

Spotlights

Spotlights are flexible in their positioning, so the last step in doing any display is to reset the lights so they are highlighting the proper areas of the display. Colored filters may be used on the spotlights to create various effects, such as using a blue filter to achieve a cool mood in a display. The use of colored lights or filters will have an effect on the apparent color of the merchandise.

LIGHTING INTENSITY

It is best to underlight rather than overlight. Glare must be eliminated, especially in windows and in cases where the glass will reflect the light. In stores wishing to save money and conserve energy, lighting is held to a minimum. This means that lights in the windows do not come on until dusk and then go off as soon as the store is closed. This creates a challenge for visual merchandising people in that windows must be made as effective and eye-catching as if they had lights in them.

COLOR

Color is a very potent tool for the visual merchandiser, both for use in displays as well as in general store design. Color can be utilized to identify areas or shops within the store itself. For example, a junior-dress department would be painted in bright young colors, while a designer-dress salon would use softer, more sophisticated colors. This type of color-coding of departments within the store gives the customer instant identification with the shopping area desired.

COLOR AS THEME

Color is important in visual merchandising, for it is the easiest way to register a theme or promotion with the customer. For example, color could coordinate an exterior and interior display using a "Strawberry Treat" theme and incorporating all the various shades of red, green, and white in the merchandise so that it relates to the strawberry motif.

COLOR FOR IMPACT

Color can provide impact for normally dull merchandise. The towel wall shown in the illustration is vibrant and dynamic in its presentation of regular solid-color towels which, if shown

SPECTRUM COLORS

separately, would mean nothing to the customer. This arrangement of towels according to a color spectrum allows the customer to view all the colors at one time as well as being visually confronted with this predominant presentation as she enters the department.

COLOR FOR MOOD

Color can be used to create a specific mood. For example, bedroom furniture can be given a very Victorian feeling by using a platform that has been color-coordinated to the merchandise and creating a sheeting background that would pick up the subtle pinks and greens in the fabric in the armoire, the chair, and the flowers on the table.

Color-Coordinated Merchandise

Colors can be subtle. The mood and color of the background panel is repeated in dresses on the mannequins. Delicate shadings of rose in dresses could be used as the main color in the background panel. This acts to unify the display.

ABSENCE OF COLOR

The absence of color can make an effective statement to the customer. The use of the neutrals, black and white, can be startling in their simplicity and lack of a color. The same type of effect can be softened by the addition of a green background and soft ferns. *Black and white are forceful in their starkness and have to be handled with great care.* Too much white in a display will cause it to be cold and to separate the merchandise, while an overabundance of black will result in a very heavy-looking display.

Black and White Display

Display artists must first consider the colorations of the merchandise and the packaging that is to be used. From here they can build a color story that will register with the customer.

COLOR SCHEMES

There are four basic color schemes that will put the message across:

1. Complementary
2. Analogous
3. Triadic
4. Monochromatic

A complementary color scheme is composed of any two colors which are directly opposite on the color wheel, such as red and green.

An analogous color scheme is composed of two or more colors which are adjacent on the color wheel, such as yellow, yellow-green, and green. This is a more subtle color scheme in that the colors blend with each other and present a softer color story because of their close family relationship.

The triadic color scheme is composed of three colors which are equidistant on the color wheel, such as red, blue, and yellow. The use of each color is not limited to one-third of the display, but rather to the amount of merchandise and the background that is suitable for each color. In this display the red predominates because of the stripes in the bathrobe and shower curtain and the bright-red towels.

A monochromatic color scheme is the use of one color such as red with the varying shades and tints of that hue. The illustration shows this with all the merchandise being in the red family. This display tells a red story and a dress story.

COLOR ACCENTS

In any of the color schemes, white and black may be used as accents. White is used to separate merchandise and add relief from other colors. It adds freshness and vitality to the display. Black is used sparingly to accent items and to add visual weight to a display.

THE PSYCHOLOGICAL EFFECT OF COLOR

Colors have psychological overtones and have certain associations for different people. In general, consumer preference for colors is as follows, going from most to least preferred: blue, red, green, violet, orange, yellow. General associations with certain colors are that *blue* is a restful color which reminds the customer of the sky and the ocean. *Red* is the most vibrant color and the best for attention-getting. It is a traditional color in its association with Christmas and Valentine's day. It provides a bright accent for otherwise dull displays. *Green* is the color for spring. It is the color of nature and is very popular at present due to the orientation toward ecology and a more natural environment. *Violet* is limited in its use due to its dark and dull quality. *Orange* is as dramatic as red and must be used with care. It is traditionally associated with Hallowe'en. *Yellow* is another fun color in that it is bright and cheerful. All of these colors have various tints and shades which may be used in conjunction with the regular hue.

COLOR EFFECT SUMMARY

Blue — restful

Red — vibrant; attention-getting

Green — nature; spring

Violet — sombre, dull

Orange — dramatic, attention-getting, Hallowe'en

Yellow — bright, cheerful

Color is probably the most important component the visual merchandiser has to work with because it is inherent in each piece of merchandise, each prop, and each fixture. Color can be altered through presentation, by various combinations, and through selected types of lighting. Color is the one quality that will attract the customer to a display. All humans are sensitive to color and react to it. It is the job of the visual merchandiser to elicit the correct psychological reaction from the consumer through an understanding and manipulation of color.

FOR REVIEW AND DISCUSSION

1. If visual merchandising is an art form, how does it compare with other recognized art forms?
2. How can the success of a display be measured?
3. What are the three basic display formats?
4. When is the zigzag format especially valuable?
5. Compare the different feelings produced by a curved line and a straight line.
6. Give an example of how an artificial texture might be added to a display.

7. Describe the difference between the actual weight and optical weight of a piece of merchandise.

8. How would you describe symmetrical or formal balance?

9. How does informal balance differ from formal balance?

10. How would you describe dominance as it relates to merchandise displays?

11. Why is fluorescent-tube lighting generally used in a modern store?

12. Concerning lighting intensity, what is a good general rule to observe?

13. Describe how color-coding might be used to identify specific shops and areas within a store.

14. Give an example of how color might be used to create a mood.

15. What is meant by a monochromatic color scheme?

16. Give the typical psychological feeling generated by the following colors: blue, red, green, violet, orange, and yellow.

unit 6

The Structure of a Visual-Merchandising Department

The visual-merchandising department is the entity in a large, multi-unit department store which is responsible for the planning, scheduling, and executing of all the various displays, trims, and related promotions within the main store as well as the branch stores. All the display areas within the store are under the jurisdiction of this department. This is the department which projects the image of the store and presents it to the customer in all phases, from shopping bags to window displays.

To accomplish this vital task there is a formal organization with structured job classifications and responsibilities. This type of organization is necessary because it facilitates the accomplishment of store goals that lone individuals would find impossible.

The structure of a visual-merchandising department in a department store which often includes a main store and branches is the most inclusive in terms of people, jobs, and auxiliary personnel.

EXECUTIVE ORGANIZATION

SENIOR VICE PRESIDENT FOR SALES PROMOTION AND VISUAL MERCHANDISING

The person who heads the visual-merchandising department is the *Senior Vice President for Sales Promotion and Visual Merchandising.* He or she is an idea and resource person. At this high executive level he or she interacts closely with the Executive Vice President for Merchandising and Sales Promotion and the Director of Advertising and Public Relations. It is his/her responsibility to develop the themes for the trims and storewide promotions. He/she works in conjunction with others in the visual-merchandising department to give direction to the people at the lower echelons. The Senior Vice President for Sales Promotions and Visual Merchandising makes the ultimate decision in matters relating to visual merchandising.

TYPICAL STRUCTURE OF THE VISUAL MERCHANDISING DEPARTMENT

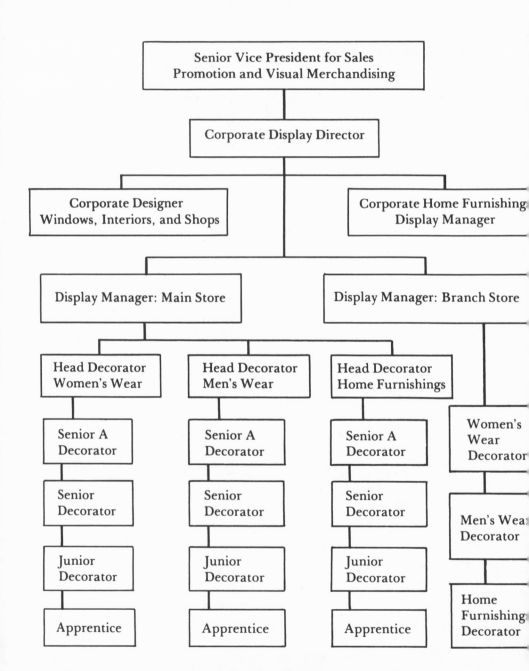

THE CORPORATE DISPLAY DIRECTOR

The Corporate Display Director reports directly to the Senior Vice President for Sales Promotion and Visual Merchandising. The term "corporate" refers to the fact that this person fills the display-director role of the executive team and is also at an executive level in the parent corporation of any allied stores. This person is directly responsible for the day-to-day operation of the department as well as long-range planning. The director will be in the market frequently, both in the domestic central markets and throughout the world, Europe and the Orient. The Corporate Display Director will research new resources and keep pace with the constantly-changing materials and products available. This research is usually done in conjunction with the Vice President. The director makes periodic visits to the branch stores to keep abreast of the presentations being done by the branch manager and his staff. The Director periodically tours the main store to accomplish the same objective. It is the Corporate Display Director who is the pivot person in the department who must interpret the direction initiated by the Vice President and communicate it to his or her people. The job of communicating and communicating effectively is of the utmost importance in visual merchandising because of the variety and number of people involved in each presentation. The Director should be the creative and innovative inspiration for the entire department.

The Display Director must also be an adept manager of finances, for he or she is responsible for a sizable budget. To do the yearly budget, the person must have input as to the number and type of promotions planned, the number of fashion shows, as well as changes anticipated in store fixturing and layout, and any new shops or galleries that will go in. All of this has a bearing on which classifications will receive what. The display director must be as innovative and creative with financial resources as with display ideas.

There are two people who report directly to the Corporate Display Director. They are:

The Corporate Designer for Windows, Interiors, and Shops
The Corporate Home-Furnishings Display Manager

These two people take the ideas and the directives of the

Vice President and the Director and oversee their design and execution.

THE CORPORATE DESIGNER

The corporate designer has the responsibility of designing shops within the store such as a shoe salon, a dress boutique, or a casual china shop, either alone or with the aid of manufacturers' representatives. The designer also works closely with the Store Planning Department on interior colors, wallpaper and fixtures. He or she works from the submitted window schedule and designs the layout and the backgrounds for the windows. Actual layouts are done and sent to the branch stores to insure a uniform presentation. The designer is frequently in the markets with the director. He or she shops both the display resources and merchandise resources to be aware of the type of merchandise that designing will be done for.

THE CORPORATE HOME-FURNISHINGS DISPLAY MANAGER

The Corporate Home-Furnishings Display Manager is responsible for all the home-furnishings areas in all of the stores. This involves all interior displays, special promotions, and windows. This person spends much time in the branch stores aiding the people there in the interpretations of his or her directives. The Home-Furnishings Display Manager researches both markets, display, and merchandise, for inspiration as well as information. Working closely with the Home Furnishings Fashion Coordinator assures that the newest, most fashionable merchandise is being promoted. This person is directly responsible for the execution and follow-through on the ideas and directions which come from the director and the Vice President.

In some stores there will be an equivalent of the Corporate Home-Furnishings Display Manager for the ready-to-wear areas of the store. This person would have the same responsibilities and functions except that they would all be related to ready-to-wear.

The four persons previously mentioned, Senior Vice President for Sales Promotion and Visual Merchandising, Corporate

Display Director, Corporate Designer for Windows, Interiors, and Shops, and the Corporate Home-Furnishings Display Manager, are all at the executive level both in the main store itself and the parent organization. The next level involves the managers of the individual stores and their respective staffs.

MAIN-STORE ORGANIZATION

The main store and the branch stores operate in a similar manner with the exception being that the main store is much larger and therefore necessitates a much larger staff to maintain it.

DISPLAY MANAGER

The main store has a display manager who is responsible for the entire store, both ready-to-wear and home furnishings. This person receives direction from the executive level, interprets it, assigns specific personnel to specific duties, and follows through on their execution. Here again the important qualities of a display manager are the ability to communicate effectively, work with people of various backgrounds and artistic temperment, and follow through on a project until it is completed. The presence of the display manager throughout the store is vital at all times, for store personnel depend upon him or her for guidance and knowledge. The display manager must be an aware individual with a mind for detail and an ability to notice everything. This person has a large staff to help with these many duties.

THE WORKING SUPERVISOR

There is a working supervisor for each of the three areas: women's wear, men's wear, and home furnishings. These people have the title of Head Decorator, which indicates they have a record of long service and experience in the field. They receive the work assignments from the display manager and assign their subordinates to the various jobs. They act in the role of a foreman in that they oversee the various displays being done as well as working themselves. The staff under the head decorator has various designations according to length of service and experience.

DECORATORS

A person who has had three-to-four years of experience in the field and can handle certain responsibilities will have the title of *Senior A Decorator*. A person with two-to-three years experience who does not have the responsibilities of a Senior A Decorator will be classified as a *Senior Decorator*. *A Junior Decorator* is a person with one-to-two years of experience in the field. The term *decorator apprentice* is given to a person who is either new in the field or has had less than a year's experience. The salary levels are commensurate with the job classification.

Decorator Duties

Each decorator will be assigned a specific floor on which to work. For example, an apprentice might have a junior dress shop or all the junior departments where the work is mainly dressing mannequins and doing accessory displays. A junior decorator could be assigned to a whole home-furnishings floor where he would have all classifications to display. The assignments correspond to the level of experience and achievement. This permits the decorator to become familiar with one area. All the decorators have to be flexible, for during times of a big display push such as Christmas, they may be pulled from their regular area to work in other departments with which they are not familiar. This serves to increase their working knowledge and improve their techniques.

BRANCH-STORE ORGANIZATION

The branch display department functions in much the same manner as the main store, but on a smaller scale, due to its size.

DISPLAY MANAGER

There is a display manager who is responsible for the entire store, both ready-to-wear and home furnishings. This person reports both to the Corporate Home Furnishings Display Manager and the Display Director. The branch-store display manager must be a flexible person capable of operating in all areas and usually on a small budget. Since there are usually fewer windows in the branch store, the display manager will follow an adaptation of the window schedule provided by the designer and the home-furnishings manager. The branch-store display manager will receive a specific window layout but still be allowed artistic freedom in its interpretation. Chain stores, on the other hand, spell out exactly where every piece of merchandise is to go and how it is to be positioned.

The branch-store manager also has freedom in regard to the store interior. Interior displays are keyed to the themes that are being used company-wide and must reflect the current trends and merchandise being featured. The display manager is free to interpret them in such a manner that a branch store will reflect the company image but will also show the personality and style of the display manager.

BRANCH-STORE STAFFING

The display manager will have a staff commensurate with the size of the store. Usually a three-floor branch store will support a staff of three (exclusive of the manager). This allows one person for women's wear, one for men's wear, and one for home furnishings.

The job of the decorator in the branch store is a little different than that of a decorator in the main store. They have to be more flexible and have larger areas to cover. They are also their own carpenters, designers, and prop makers. It is the branch store where the most creative and ingenious people are needed because of the amount of work to be done and the small budgets they must work with.

It would not be unusual to work in the men's department one day and do jewelry cases the next. The branch store is a great training ground due to the diversity of the displays undertaken.

SUPPORTIVE PERSONNEL

The visual-merchandising department does not operate in a vacuum. It must not be isolated from the rest of the store, for that is where the ideas and the merchandise come from.

Fashion Coordinator

THE FASHION COORDINATOR

In a large department store there will be a fashion co-ordinator for both ready-to-wear and home furnishings. These people are extremely important because they are on top of the latest and the newest in merchandise and merchandise presentation. It is part of their job to issue a window schedule which lists what is to go into each window. They also feed ideas on displays to the department and keep its personnel abreast of the fashion items in both areas.

HOME-FURNISHINGS COORDINATOR

If the store is on an environmental-selling basis for home furnishings, the home-furnishings coordinator will design these rooms and it will be the function of the display department to set them up and then maintain them.

SPECIAL-EVENTS DIRECTOR

The special-events director is another person who works closely with the display department. *This person is part of the advertising department but must interact with the visual-merchandising department* to carry out the promotions. The display department designs the settings for the promotions and sees to their execution.

THE CARPENTER AND SIGN SHOP

The physical work of display is supported by a carpenter shop where major projects are undertaken. A large store will also have its own sign shop which makes all the signs for all the windows, promotions, and sales in all the stores.

The display department could not operate without the myriad of people it interacts with both inside and outside of the store. The department must have input from as many sources as possible, synthesize them, rework them, and adapt them for the best interests of the store. This department, more than any other, is the image-maker of the store.

SUPPORTIVE PERSONNEL IN SMALLER STORES

As stores change in size, so do the visual-merchandising departments. In a multi-unit specialty store the structure would be similar to that of a large department store, except all home-furnishings personnel would be deleted if it is mainly a ready-to-wear store. As this type of store gets smaller, so does the staff. In a small store there would be only one display director and he would travel between the stores.

Discount houses operate on a different basis due to their self-service structure and lack of a reliance on display to sell their merchandise. They limit themselves to mass-merchandising techniques and heavy advertising. Their displays, what there is of them, are done by salespeople with a display director overseeing the advertising and promotional end of the business.

FREE-LANCE DISPLAY ARTIST

There are many stores too small to have a visual-merchandising department or even a display person. They hire a free-lance display artist who comes in on a predetermined schedule. This artist does the windows and the in-store displays. The store may provide him with a budget for props, or he may provide them and include this in his billing.

Salespeople will do the interior displays in the interim. The one disadvantage with this is that the individual's style may come through rather than a projection of the store's image. Also, if one person does several stores in an area, a customer will be able to notice a similarity in the style and feel of the displays.

Whatever the kind of store, visual merchandising is of crucial importance to the store because it is the visual merchandising department that puts the merchandise before the public and presents the store's image. A coordinated effort between all people in the department and their supportive departments is necessary for an effective presentation to the customer. This can only be accomplished through direct and open communication with each other as well as having creative, innovative and strong people at all levels.

FOR REVIEW AND DISCUSSION

1. In general, what are the responsibilities of the visual-merchandise department of a large, multi-unit department store?

2. Name some of the duties of the Senior Vice President for Sales Promotion and Visual Merchandising.

3. Why is it important that the Corporate Display Director have excellent communication skills?

4. What are the responsibilities of the Corporate Designer?

5. What are some of the personal qualifications of a main store Display Manager?

6. Why is it important that decorators become familiar with more than one area of decorating within a store?

8. Why is the Fashion Coordinator an important person in a large store?

9. Why are small stores more inclined to hire a free-lance display artist?

The Excitement and Challenge of Visual Merchandising

From its humble beginnings in the open market in primitive lands, visual merchandising has grown to fill a dominant position in the selling process. The twentieth century has seen visual merchandising assume new and added prominence in retail stores due to changing conditions in society as well as fluctuations in the economy. The visual merchandiser is constantly called upon to meet the desires and demands of the well-informed modern consumer. A modern theory of retail institutional change tells us that as a store changes and reaches maturity, it has a larger physical plant, more elaborate store fixtures and displays, and it undertakes greater promotional efforts. *At the same time "operating costs tend to rise."* At this point the job of the visual merchandiser becomes even more important in reducing the cost of selling the merchandise through more effective use of display. The visual merchandiser must also create and project the image of the store at the same time.

COORDINATION — THE KEY POINT

The exterior of the store acts as an invitation to the consumer. Once inside, the interior displays must hold the attention of the consumer and induce her to buy. The coordination between the exterior and the interior is crucial in that it must not confuse the consumer. It is also important because it creates a unified store appearance.

TOOLS OF THE VISUAL MERCHANDISER

To accomplish his tasks, the visual merchandiser has more props, fixtures, materials, and merchandise at his disposal than ever before. Plexiglass, chrome, and wood are the basic materials from which fixtures are made. New inventions in related fields such as the plastics industry, textiles, and photography find their way into visual merchandising. Holography is one such invention. It is a specialized photographic process, utilizing laser light, that can capture, in full dimensions, an original scene on a photographic film or plate.

In producing a hologram there is no lens between the subject and the camera. The entire room is the camera. The image is projected into what seems to be thin air so that the viewer can walk right through the image. A large jewelry store used this medium to suspend a $100,000 diamond bracelet from a hand in front of their establishment. There was no fear of shoplifting, for the bracelet was inside the store.

The European markets as well as the American markets are offering a wealth of materials with which to create merchandising illusions. Even with all this available, the visual merchandiser must still adhere to basic elements and principles of visual merchandising design as well as to basic facts of color and lighting.

CREATIVITY — A MUST!

The visual-merchandising department itself has grown from one window trimmer who worked at night to a large department with various personnel who perform specialized functions. The organizational structure may be stratified and complex or may be at the primary level of a free-lance display artist. Regardless of size or number of people, basic talent and native creativity are a must for a successful visual-merchandising department.

FUTURE GROWTH

The importance of visual merchandising to the whole retail function can only continue to grow. As stores reduce their sales personnel, it will be the responsibility of the visual merchandiser to bring merchandise to the public in a dignified manner even when self-selection sales are involved. Even in the discount store, the displays must be attractive and properly arranged. As costs continue to spiral upward, the added touch of creative display will be ever necessary to sell merchandise. The visual-merchandising department itself may feel budgetary problems, and, as a result, large-scale expensive promotions may decrease in number.

Props and fixtures will be purchased which are multi-purpose in nature. Total store trims will be simpler in nature and not changed as frequently. Rather, existing trims will be updated by the addition of new props. Researchers see more flexibility in the display staffs due to cutbacks in personnel. The dead wood will be eliminated in favor of productive, creative people.

THE EFFECT OF THE ECONOMY

The increase in importance of the visual-merchandising department is tied to the economy in general and to the economy of the store in particular. The visual-merchandising department that is creative both displaywise and financially will survive and grow because of its flexibility and innovativeness. The others will merely survive.

FUTURE OPPORTUNITY

The visual-merchandising field allows a creative person who is interested in business to combine the two. It allows for freedom of artistic expression within the structure of an organization. The frustrations are inherent as with any artistic endeavor, but the results are more tangible in terms of merchandise turnover and sales.

TRAINING

A few colleges offer courses in visual merchandising in their retailing program, and their goal is a comprehensive program of study to train a display artist. Several junior colleges have such programs as well. Distributive Education Programs offer training at the high-school level and a number of proprietory schools are also involved.

KNOWING THE CONSUMER

As consumers become more sophisticated, their buying habits change. From time-to-time a survey of buying habits in response to exterior and interior displays is needed to gauge the effectiveness of displays and the new methods and materials being used. Another area for survey would be the perception of the image of a store by the customer as a result of the exterior and interior displays. A third survey that would be of value would be one on the impact and registration of color in a store with the attendant customer reactions.

The field of visual merchandising is expanding rapidly and the information about it must also grow. Such information will then be of value to both the practitioners of the art and the stores that employ them.

FOR REVIEW AND DISCUSSION

1. What major challenge confronts the visual merchandiser when budgets become tight?
2. Can you think of any new inventions that might be of help to the fashion merchandiser in the future?
3. If you had an unrestricted choice of jobs in the visual-merchandising field, which one would you seek? Why?
4. In reference to the above question, make a list of your strong character points that would appear to qualify you for this position.

unit 8

An Expression of Art

As an example of matchless elegance in both image and merchandise, Tiffany's of New York is virtually unrivaled. It is, therefore, helpful and stimulating to study their philosophy and implementation of visual merchandising through their unique window displays. Tiffany windows stand out as something of a visual gift to the passerby, inviting attention with their own particular blend of subtle splendor and extraordinary good taste.

The underlying philosophy of a Tiffany window is, very simply, that it is a work of art. The Tiffany designer thinks of window displays exactly as a painter thinks, and then works hard to express each idea. The result is, inevitably, a piece of sheer artistry; and because there is nothing commercial in the thinking or planning, whatever sales result from the displays are considered frosting on the cake.

Prior to this approach of pure art, the Tiffany windows had been conventional displays of selected merchandise set against the background of a heavy mass of pleated curtains, which gave the items on display an air of Victorian stodginess. The new designer's first step was to remove the pleats, and from there to change the character of the displays from traditional exhibitions of merchandise to inspired works of art, elegant inventions that borrow elements from painting, sculpture, collage, and theater.

The inspiration for the idea, or theme, of the window is, of course, the most difficult and creative in the process of the Tiffany windows, and hand-in-hand with this process goes the selection of props. These two aspects are the most time-consuming, followed by the easier step of selection of the merchandise to go with them. Combining the two generates a relationship between the ordinary and the sublime, together with a theatrical, virtually scale-less use of the small shallow space, which has become the trademark of the Tiffany displays. Although from time to time such backgrounds as fabric, tapestries, and paintings are used, the designer prefers three-dimensional objects — sculpture, bas-relief, découpage, and found objects. The reason for this is that they usually lend themselves better to lighting, and lighting is fifty percent of the total effect. The artwork used is almost always by contemporary artists who do not have galleries: a rental fee is paid for the use and sometimes, as a bonus, the work is sold out of the window. However, the Tiffany designer's greatest delight is in using ordinary, everyday objects as a foil for the glitter of gems, crystal, and precious metal — things such as whole eggshells, parts of antique wooden molds, seashells, vines, flowers, fruit, and vegetables. Because there is such beauty to be found in ordinary things, a sense of reward must result from showing it to those who have never really seen it before.

Although any window display functions somewhat as a miniature stage on which to present something to the public, the special theatrical quality of the Tiffany windows is produced by the sometimes dramatic interaction of the unusual objects shown, as well as the designer's instinct for spatial relationships and lighting.

Tiffany's window-design staff find their task of creating five windows every two weeks a supreme challenge to creativity; and although the resources of free-lance artists' ideas are often utilized, the process of producing these special effects results from the unusual combination of creative artistry with an instinctive sense of basic merchandising.

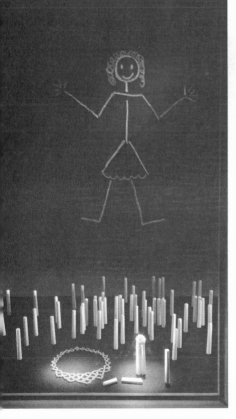

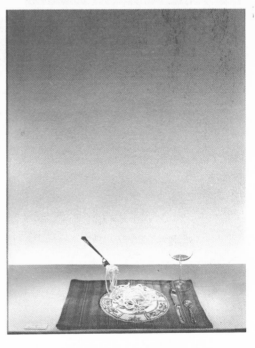

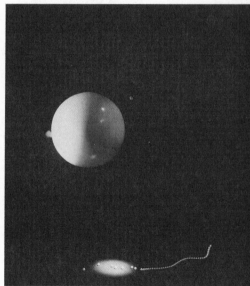

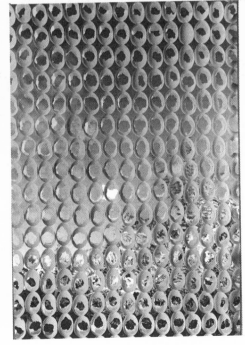

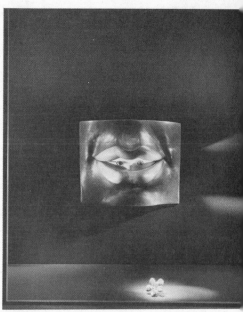

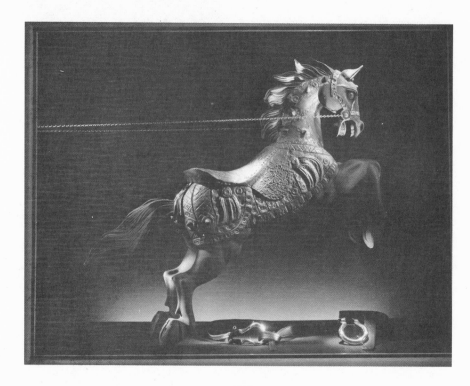

Glossary

A-frame—rectangular fixture used for hanging merchandise

aisle table—table located in the aisle of a store used as an island

analogous color scheme—any two or more colors which are adjacent on the color wheel

angled storefront—straight storefront modified with deeply-recessed doorways to create more display area

arcade storefront—straight storefront with several recessed doorways with glass islands in between them

arcade storefront

asymmetrical balance—balancing a display by means of spaces and shapes, not actual objects

asymmetrical balance

book out—to sign out merchandise for a display in a merchandise requisition book

buildup—a prop used in a display to create different levels or to raise the height of an object

case—rectangular glass-enclosed display area which utilizes small-scale merchandise such as jewelry and cosmetics

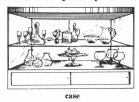

case

chain store—one of a series of stores with centralized management and tight control

complementary color scheme—any two colors which are opposite each other on the color wheel

corner window—most important window in a storefront due to its two-sided exposure at the intersection of two traffic patterns

corner window

discount house—departmentalized retail establishment utilizing self-service to sell general merchandise on a low-profit/high-turnover basis

draper—forerunner of modern discounters in that they cut price and use promotional advertising

elevated window—exterior display window raised 12-18 inches up from sidewalk level

elevated window

elevator window—exterior display window that is raised and lowered mechanically

environmental setting—three-sided full-scale room display which simulates a home environment

environmental setting

fixture—any item used to display or hold merchandise

foam core—light-weight board consisting of a sandwich of porous polystyrene foam covered on both sides with white clay paper

focal point—the point of interest in a display to which the eye is drawn by various techniques

form—full and partial body structures of males and females used to display ready-to-wear

free-flow layout—store layout which considers the requirements of the departments and is not symmetrical

free-flow layout

full-service department store—departmentalized retailing establishment which carries both ready-to-wear and home furnishings

gondola—rectangular fixture on which merchandise is either stacked or laid

gridiron plan—symmetrical store layout where store is divided into sections by aisles that run straight from front to back

gridiron plan

head—representation of the human head in styrofoam or plastic used to display wigs and millinery

holography—special photographic process, utilizing laser light, that can capture in full dimensions an original scene on a photographic film or plate

institutional window — noncommercial window display used to promote goodwill

island area—stationary display platform

ledge—display area recessed into the wall above a set of shelves. Also, the display area on the top of a center unit in a selling area

line-of-goods window—window display using all the same classification of merchandise

line-of-goods window

lobby window—exterior display window found in a store with either an angled or arcade front

mannequin—full-figure form of a man, woman, or child made from various materials

merchandise - requisition book—sign - out book for merchandise to be used in displays

monochromatic color scheme—any one color and the various shades and tints of that hue

no-seam paper—solid color durable paper, nine feet wide, used primarily for backgrounds in display windows

no-seam paper

one-item window—exterior display window showing only one piece of merchandise

open-backed window—exterior display window without a back which allows a view into the store

pad—piece of foam core cut to fit into the bottom of a case

pinning—procedure of altering a garment, with common pins, to fit a mannequin without physically changing it

pinning

platform—raised free-standing display area

promotional window—sale window

promotional window

prop—an item used to add interest and uniqueness to a display which is not for sale

pyramid format—display arrangement where the base is broad and the merchandise is built up to one point

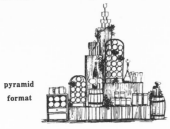

pyramid
format

ramped window—window with a floor which is higher in the back than the front

related - merchandise window—exterior display window in which all the merchandise is related by theme, color, style, etc.

related - merchandise window

round—circular fixture used for hanging merchandise

signing—the logo scrolls used in windows to identify the promotion or theme

shadow box—enclosed display area used for small items

shadow box

shopboard—the bottom of a window parallel to the ground; archaic

specialty store—retail organization characterized by high degree of specialization in merchandise classifications

stand—display fixture with multiple attachments

step format—window arrangement with a gradation in levels from lowest to highest with all levels parallel

straight storefront—front of store which is parallel to the sidewalk

straight storefront

symmetrical balance—formal balance accomplished by duplication of objects on each side of an imaginary central axis

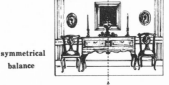

symmetrical
balance

torso—form which duplicates the areas of the body from the neck to the pelvis without appendages

torso

triadic color scheme—any three colors which are equidistant on the color wheel

trim—the seasonal theme or motif used throughout a store

T-stand—fixture in the shape of a T used to hang a limited number of garments

visual merchandising—the art of effective merchandise presentation

weight—the apparent, not actual weight of an object due to its physical appearance

window schedule—outline of timing and merchandise for window changes

window trimmer—the original term for a display person originating around 1900

zigzag—display arrangement with a broad base which builds up to several points through the use of steps

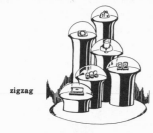

zigzag

Cross Index

N

O

P

R

S